D1311610

CANADA
The Missing Years

CANADA
The Missing Years

THE LOST IMAGES OF OUR HERITAGE
· 1895-1924 ·

Windsor Public Library

PATRICIA PIERCE

Stoddart

Dedication

To May Willoughby Fell,
born in Toronto in 1900.

TITLE PAGE
"The beach at Kelowna looking towards the Grandstand and Aquatic Building."
G. H. E. HUDSON, 1910.

FRONT ENDPAPER
Winnipeg in 1912, a detail from a panoramic view.
See also pages 86 and 87.

Copyright © 1985 by Patricia Pierce

All rights reserved. No part of this publication may be
reproduced, stored in a retrieval system, or transmitted, in any
form or by any means, electronic, mechanical, photocopying,
recording or otherwise, without the prior permission of
Hamlyn Publishing and the copyright holder.

First published in 1985 by
Stoddart Publishing Co. Limited
34 Lesmill Road
Don Mills, Ontario, Canada
M3B 2TC

First published in the United Kingdom by Hamlyn Publishing

CANADIAN CATALOGUING IN PUBLICATION DATA

Pierce, Pat
Canada: the missing years 1895–1924

Includes index.
ISBN: 0–7737–2052–9

1. Canada – History – 1867–1914 – Pictorial works
2. Canada – History – 1914–1945 – Pictorial works
3. Canada – Description and travel – 1868–1900 – Views.
4. Canada – Description and travel – 1901–1950 – Views.
I. Title.

FC540.P53 1985   971.05′022′2   C85–098554–4
F1034.P53 1985

Printed and bound in Italy

CONTENTS

"Chief Duckhunter, a Canadian Indian of Victoria."
A. W. GELSTON, 1913.

6

INTRODUCTION

The Story of the Canadian Collection at the British Library in London

A Canadian university professor has stumbled upon what will almost certainly prove to be the largest and best collection of Canadian material anywhere outside of Canada for the period 1895 to 1924. The vast extent of this collection at the British Library in London had been unrealized, although parts of it were catalogued. In 1979 when Dr Patrick O'Neill began searching for unknown Canadian plays at the British Library, he found 300 unrecorded plays – and a collection of some 40,000 items, including 2,500 maps, 10,000 books, 11,000 pieces of sheet music, 4,000 photographs, and much more. This is the story of that collection and, more importantly, the story of Canada in photographs taken during the period when the new nation – full of hope and promise – was emerging.

In pursuit of his great love – Canadian drama – Dr O'Neill spent his holidays searching, with considerable success, for unrecorded Canadian plays. Earlier in 1979 he had found about 1,000 plays, for the most part unknown, at the Library of Congress in Washington. In manuscript form, some were too brittle to handle; however, almost 800 were microfilmed by the Library of Congress D.C. for the Library at Mount Saint Vincent – Dr O'Neill's university – a generous act of Canadian-American friendship.

Back in 1976 Dr O'Neill had begun looking for new sources of Canadian plays. During holidays before Christmas he went to the National Library, the Public Archives of Canada, and Consumer and Corporate Affairs in Ottawa, but most of the material prior to 1924 was missing. A modest man, who says that he has done nothing extraordinary – simply followed normal research techniques – he then decided to look closely at the various Canadian Copyright Acts. He soon discovered that between the years 1895 and 1924, the Canadian government was compelled by law to send one copy of all material deposited at Ottawa to register copyright to the Library of the British Museum, now the British Library, in London. There were two other copies for Ottawa, one for the Copyright Office and one for the Library of Parliament.

This edict – reinforcing one dating back to 1842 that had been ignored – was hotly debated in the Canadian House of Commons at the time, but was fortunately complied with. British diplomatic channels had helped achieve this result and so increased the resources of the British Museum Library.

The Canadians had their own motives for complying. They hoped that by placating the British on this point, the latter would support them in passing a new copyright act which would legally allow Canadian publishers to pirate US material, that is, to use copyrighted material without paying any fees. Pirating was widespread in the nineteenth century and highly organized. For example, some Ontario publishers had printing plants just over the border in Buffalo, where books were manufactured to be sold in Canada. In the 1880s when visiting Montreal, Mark Twain had delivered a scathing attack on Canadian publishers for bypassing US copyright regulations. The Canadians never achieved their aim, and the act had a much more commendable, but unexpected, outcome.

The new ruling applied to all of Britain's colonies. Faced with diplomatic pressure, Canada, luckily, complied. Newfoundland, then a separate colony, unfortunately didn't, nor did Australia, much to the regret of present-day historians in that country.

For, because of a remarkable sequence of events, the British Library collection of Canadian copyright material is the most complete of the three sets that has survived for the period 1895 to 1924.

What happened to the two Canadian sets? The set at the Library of Parliament was almost completely destroyed in two fires, and much of the set at the Copyright Office was thrown out.

Fire was a common hazard in the early years of this century, and important buildings were not immune. Not one fire at the Library of Parliament in Ottawa, but two, destroyed part of that set. The first fire in 1916 actually started in the Library itself, and went on to destroy the rest of the Parliament buildings. The extent of the damage is revealed in the Report of the Joint Librarians:

> The disastrous fire which destroyed the Parliament Buildings, in February, did not leave the Library unscathed.

The fire originated in the reading room, which contained a large and valuable collection of books, as well as the current newspapers.

When these took fire, the whole collection of books was hopelessly doomed to destruction.

During the night, the water thrown upon the burning buildings found its way ultimately to the Library, and the floor was flooded to the depth of many inches, during the two days which followed.

Much damage was done by the flood of water; but owing to the exertions of some members of the Library staff, who were on duty, the books on the lower shelves were, as far as time allowed, removed and placed on higher shelves. (*British Library Occasional Papers, 1 Canadian Studies*, 1984)

In 1953 the second fire started in the dome of the Library of Parliament. Water cascading down on the collection caused most of the damage, as it had done with the 1916 fire.

As for the set at the Copyright Office, forces other than acts of nature were at work. A memorandum of 1937 has been located in which the Copyright Office requested advice on what to do with its enormous collection of deposit material, pending a move to an office with inadequate storage space. In 1938 the Committee of the Privy Council responded that few of the "several thousands of volumes of books, catalogues, periodicals, pamphlets, sheet music, maps" and so on were of any value.

The result was a decision which appals Canadian historians today. Governor-General Lord Tweedsmuir and Prime Minister MacKenzie King signed an order-in-council which decreed that the material be offered to the Secretary of State Library, and that the Copyright Office dispose of what remained. It is recorded that "One hundred and fifty-five books of prominent Canadian statesmen and the history of Canada were obtained from the Copyright Office, together with some sixty volumes of Canadian fiction" and deposited

in the Secretary of State Library. Mystery attends the fate of the rest of the collection. While it seems that no record exists today, some 2,500 photographs were eventually found in the Public Archives. Of the remaining 37,000-odd items, no mention is made. We can only presume that they were destroyed or given away.

In time new collections were begun, and the collection at the British Library was forgotten, as was the entire episode.

When Dr O'Neill travelled to the British Library for the first time in 1979, he was most hopeful of finding some undiscovered Canadian plays, an idea he relished. With the dedication of a man who has named his two sons after Irish playwights, he read through the entire

eight volumes of the "Canadian Copyright Receipt Book" (mainly hand-written notes), recording copyright material received from 1895 to 1924. He was the first Canadian to look at these volumes. It was clear that, not only were there new plays, but that they were only a small part of a vast deposit of Canadian material in the British Library. Although much of it was catalogued, thousands of items were not, and no one before had realized the *extent* of the vast collection. As Dr O'Neill points out, unless catalogues and bibliographies are compiled, academics and researchers cannot even be aware of the existence of material which would be useful to them.

He returned to Canada and informed Norman Horrocks, Director, School of Library Service,

"Canadian Parliament Buildings Destroyed by Fire, February 3, 1916." It was in this fire, which began in the Library (centre back), that some Canadian copyright material was destroyed. Seven people died in the fire. The photograph upper left shows Parliament's temporary meeting place.

MONTREAL STANDARD PUBLISHING CO., LTD., 1916.

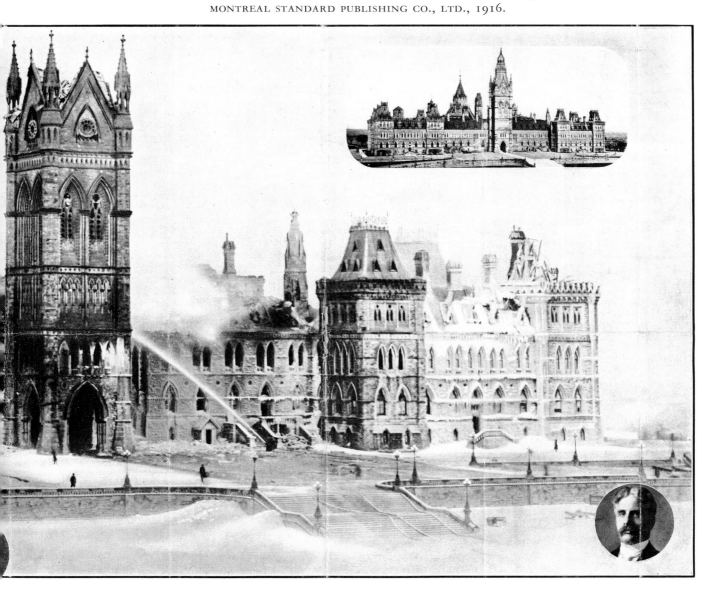

Dalhousie University, of the collection at the British Library. At the same time he wrote to the National Library and the Public Archives of Canada in Ottawa, telling them of his find. Events would prove that the copyright collections of the National Library and the Public Archives were greatly surpassed by the British Library Canadian Collection for the period 1895 to 1924.

In the 1970s no money was available from Canadian government sources for the compilation of bibliographies. Following publication of the *Symons Report* and the setting up of the Canada Council Consultative Group on University Research in 1975, several Canadians had begun to campaign for Canadian funding for the compilation of bibliographies, which would be invaluable for locating Canadiana. Among the most active campaigners were Professor Francess Halpenny, University of Toronto and General Editor, the *Dictionary of Canadian Biography/Dictionnaire biographique du Canada*, and Professor Anne B. Piternick, School of Librarianship, University of British Columbia. Such efforts were rewarded when the Social Sciences and Humanities Research Council of Canada (SSHRCC) in 1981 set up The Canadian Studies Research Program "to improve access to sources for research in Canadian studies by cataloguing and indexing existing repository or thematic collections of interest to researchers."

In April 1982 Dr O'Neill received a SSHRCC grant from this funding to find, identify and list Canadian material in the British Library. Work on the Canadian Collection at the British Library began in 1983. Dr O'Neill, his wife Dianne, and their two sons, St John and Brendan, moved to England for a period of fourteen months. Dr O'Neill was assisted by Researcher Margaret Cooter, a Dalhousie graduate who also moved to England. Following Dr O'Neill's return to Canada, Professor John R. T. Ettlinger, School of Library Service, Dalhousie University, supervised the research for five months until he withdrew from the project because of other commitments. In 1984 Researcher Barbara James, a graduate of and former Librarian at Dalhousie, moved to England and took over from Margaret Cooter. To the end of 1984, the project received approximately $90,000 from SSHRCC funding.

Patrick O'Neill tells us that it took the first year of the project just to find everything, let alone begin to index it. He approached the staff librarians at the British Library for clues as to where to look for the photographs he felt sure were there. He was told that the British Library does not keep photographs. Therefore there could not be any photographs. After five weeks of strong denials, he was finally advised to ask some of the old guard among the staff if they could remember where the Canadian material might have been deposited. Philip Harris (then Head, West European Branch), who had been at the Library for over forty years, eventually suggested the Woolwich Arsenal, an annex of the Library.

British Library deposits are stored in twenty-three buildings, three of which are warehouses at Woolwich Arsenal. An immense amount of material had been moved there from the burgeoning basements of the British Library about twelve years previously. Known as the "Colonial dump", it is but one of several repositories used by the Library for uncatalogued material.

On 13 October 1982, in one of these vast warehouses, "on the second floor, in the far corner", Dr O'Neill and Margaret Cooter found over 4,000 pieces of Canadiana, mainly photographs and trade material. This "dump" occupied about 90 metres (300 linear feet) of shelving and everything was covered with layers of dust. Mixed up with the Canadian material were British items and a few odds and ends from Malta, Australia and the USA.

The photographs were in reasonably good condition because they had been handled so little. Other than the move to Woolwich, and three moves in four years at Woolwich, they had not been touched for decades. Some of the photographs were found standing on end, some were in loose piles, some were slipped into books. Most were unprotected. There were even four enormous rolls of photographs – each roll about one foot wide and containing about 30 or 40 of the very long military photographs taken before the units left Canada for the European battlefields of the First World War. Sometimes books had been placed on top of these rolls, resulting in cracks in the photographs. They were left for the Conservation Officer at the British Library to unroll.

Now the work began of cleaning and organizing them. Each photograph was dusted with cheesecloth provided by the British Library, placed in its own acid-free envelope, also provided, and the envelope was marked with the original reference number. Following the original copyright deposit list, an index card was filled out for each photograph received all those years ago. The card was then matched up with each newly-found photograph – work which took weeks. When a photograph was located, its measurements and any additional information were also noted on the card.

The photographs were eventually taken to the office of James Egles, English Language Branch, British Library Reference Division, and there they remained under his knowledgeable and watchful eye until incorporated into the system.

There are other Canadian photographs at the British Library, which are part of the entire Canadian Collection. Some are in the Map Library, including more than 1,000 scenographic photographs. There is always an element of surprise when referring to the collection. Calling up an index number might bring a single photograph, a batch of 400 photographs, an album or book of photographs, or panoramic views, singly or in multiples, and each of these may be two and a half or three metres (eight or ten feet) long! The latter result was apparently achieved by joining up a series of photographs, although the joins are usually imperceptible.

Dr O'Neill discovered the photographs in the Map Library when preparing the inventory of the Canadian map collection, which necessitated reading the entire Map Catalogue – thousands of entries. This led to the simultaneous discovery of the Goad Insurance Plans, photographs, and books. These items have now been indexed.

In addition, there are 1,700 First World War photographs in the main library, which have already been copied for the Public Archives of Canada. Then, there are about 120 photographs of native peoples, more than half taken by Geraldine Moodie, in the Museum of Mankind, formerly the Department of Ethnography of the British Museum. They have also been copied for the Public Archives of Canada. In all, the researchers have located about 3,500 of the 5,000 photographs believed to have been sent to the Library.

The majority of the photographs in this book are from the collection discovered at Woolwich Arsenal by Dr O'Neill and over half are not available in the remains of the other two sets in the Public Archives in Ottawa. A sampling of them was first displayed at a Colloquium on the British Library Collections and Canadian Studies held at the British Library in August 1983. Dianne O'Neill, with a Ph.D. in Theatre, and degrees in Art History and Anthropology was most aptly qualified to make the selection of the fifty photographs for this exhibition, some of which are included here.

Although the photographs are perhaps the most immediately appealing of the 40,000 or so items in the whole collection, the newly discovered 1,300 Charles E. Goad Ltd Insurance Plans have an undeniable fascination of their own. These fire insurance plans show communities in great detail at a certain point in time. Sometimes the plans were redrawn, say at ten-year intervals, so one can see how a community developed. Symbols and colour coding were used to show the outside and inside construction of buildings, which buildings were insured by Goad, fire hazards, and so on. Intriguing details emerge on close examination: a

map of Vancouver at the turn-of-the-century clearly indicates "opium dens". Of these 1,300 plans, less than 500 exist in Canada.

There are about 10,000 books in the collection, of which only about 3,000 are listed in Canadian bibliographies. Along with the photographs, the maps and the insurance plans, Margaret Cooter catalogued the books among the new material.

Of the 11,000 pieces of sheet music, the number already known in Canada is yet to be determined. The sheet music was largely uncatalogued and unlisted, leaving a mammoth task for Dr O'Neill and Barbara James, who worked on the material full time. There was only one way to do it. Barbara systematically opened and checked every bundle – there were thousands of bundles. This alone took five months of work in the dark and airless "Pen 4". "Pen 4" is one of the numerous locked enclosures similar to cages, which are used for storing valuable material. They are located off a labyrinth of corridors tucked away behind the magnificent walls of the British Library's famous Reading Room. "Pen 4" was where the Canadian sheet music was found, hidden among sheet music from all over the world. Sheet music at that time was printed on poor quality pulp paper with a high acidic content and excessive handling would have destroyed it, so the dusty hiding place served a useful purpose.

The British Library has always had some Canadian material in its collections, which of course was already documented. Postage stamps and books are but two examples. The previously catalogued material combined with the newly discovered material make the collection unusually well rounded, as does the wealth of ephemera – those trivial items that weren't usually collected – such as puzzles, games, postcards, individual poems, and greeting cards, in the new collection.

There are also directories – one entry in the British Library Catalogue to cover hundreds of directories – and trade and advertising material.

Trade material is missing from before 1915. The exact reason is unknown. There are two theories as to what became of it. One suggestion is that from 1905 trade material was no longer accepted by the Library, and that what had accumulated was pulped in 1914 or 1915 for the war effort. Perhaps more likely, Canadian trade material disappeared on 10 May 1941 when dozens of incendiary bombs fell on the British Museum. The ensuing fires in the south-west quadrant destroyed some 200,000 volumes. Among Canadian copyright material which vanished on that day were texts on law, stenography and cookery. The uncatalogued trade material was probably there too.

For the most part – from 23 July 1895, when the first

shipment arrived – the collection of Canadiana at the British Library in London is remarkably complete. One of the few gaps is revealed in the unpublished "Canadian Copyright Lists" for 1895 to 1924. Carefully noted is the fact that those items registered for copyright between 14 and 19 May 1914 had not been received. They were presumably lost when the *Empress of Ireland* sank in the St Lawrence River on 30 May.

Dr O'Neill, Associate Professor of Speech and Drama at Mount Saint Vincent University, has compiled *Canadian Copyright Deposits in the British Library, Vol. I: Maps* and *Vol. II: Insurance Plans*. To follow is *Vol. III: Directories*. These, and subsequent indexes, published by The School of Library Service, Dalhousie University, Halifax, Nova Scotia, will give access to much of the material.

And so the collection that began when section 10 of the Canadian Copyright Act of 1875 was amended in 1895 – requiring one set of Canadian copyright material to be sent to the British Library – sadly ended on 1 January 1924, when, confusingly, the Canadian Copyright Act of 1921 was finally proclaimed law. From that date the British Library lost its right to receive free copies of Canadiana. As Dr O'Neill explains in his article "Canadiana deposited in the British Museum Library between 1895 and 1924" (*British Library Occasional Papers, 1 Canadian Studies*), the situation greatly worsened with the new Act. Copies of books and other material were *not* required to be deposited to register copyright, even in Canada. This decision was reversed for Canada in 1931. Nevertheless, there are many gaps in the collections of the National Library of Canada and the Public Archives of Canada, making the British Library Canadian Collection even more valuable. In the words of Dr O'Neill: "All Canadians should be thankful that the British Library has preserved our heritage."

Among the estimated 30 million items at the British Library, the missing Canadian Collection lay unrecorded, forgotten, hidden – and safe – for decades, awaiting the time when its scope and character could be appreciated by a mature Canada, eager to assess and value a full and vital past.

Canada in the Years 1895 to 1924

This extraordinary collection of photographs has cut through an exciting, and critical, period of Canadian history. The years between 1895 and 1924 were a time of momentous change during which Canada emerged from its cocoon of an immense and loyal, but weak, colony to spread its wings as a proud and strong independent country.

In the year 1895 the confederation of the first four provinces was a mere twenty-eight years in the past and the contemporary provincial map of Canada was still far from being fully formed. The young country was determinedly struggling to establish its own identity when in 1895 the Colonial Office in London demanded the right to have a set of all material deposited for copyright in Ottawa.

It was an exciting time, too, in the history of photography, as the full potential of this invention had only shortly before been fully realized. By 1890 George Eastman's Kodak, a rollfilm camera which could be purchased for $25 with film for 100 exposures and was simple to operate, brought photography within reach of the masses, as both subjects and photographers. Flashlight powder had been invented in the 1880s, encouraging, seemingly, every family in the country to have their portraits taken against a painted scenic backdrop. Various types of photography overlapped and were in use at the same time, as the public experimented with this wonderful new toy.

On the political scene Sir John A. MacDonald, the first Prime Minister, had kept the vast country together by the force of his own personality and the use of patronage – "the glue of nationhood" – in government jobs. He had won the March 1891 election on the theme "The Old Man, The Old Flag, The Old Policy", but was soon dead – worn out by his years of struggle to securely establish the new country.

Then came the Laurier years (1893–1911) when the Liberalism of Sir Wilfred Laurier coincided with an economic boom. The increasingly confident country looked proudly to its own identity. Laurier's words "The twentieth century shall be the century of Canada and of Canadian development" were immediately shortened by the press to the exuberant "The Twentieth Century Belongs to Canada". Few doubted the truth of these words.

Laurier is the most dominant individual to appear in the collection of photographs as a whole. The Prime Minister, a French-Canadian, encouraged a spirit of compromise in meshing together the French and English heritages in Canada, not necessarily to the complete satisfaction of either, but in a way that enabled the country to move ahead smoothly.

Writers and artists were experimenting with national themes and styles, and Canadian history suddenly became a subject worthy of study and research. Photography, too, generated much interest and discussion as to whether it was or was not an art form. The advocates of "naturalist photography" were set against those who preferred soft-focus impressionistic work and formed the pictorialist movement.

By 1886 the country was bound together by tracks of steel, for the transcontinental railway now crossed the country from coast to coast. Construction had finally got under way in 1881 and the immense difficulties were overcome, mainly due to the dynamic management of William Van Horne, who became President of the Canadian Pacific Railway. This railway, with considerable foresight, made use of the camera by commissioning a number of photographers to record the sights and developments along the line, and the photographers were given special cars to accomodate their equipment and darkroom facilities. The resulting photographs were sent to Britain and Europe to provide another stimulus for the massive wave of immigration which soon followed the opening of the railway.

In 1895 the pressing issues of the day were the Manitoba Schools Question – whether or not children should be taught in the French language in a province which then had a substantial French-speaking population – and the tariff protection policy, rather than a free trade, of immense interest to farmers and manufacturers.

Gradually the country was achieving self-government in external affairs. Laurier had attended the Colonial Conference in London in 1897, the year of Queen Victoria's Diamond Jubilee, where he argued for Canadians to be involved in decisions that would affect them. He tried to avoid firm commitments of troops in foreign wars like the South African War (1889), leaving individuals to decide by "the silken bond of sentiment". In this war more than 7,000 Canadians volunteered to serve in the British Army – and largely at British expense, an event recorded in these photographs.

To assert Canada's autonomy within the Empire the first steps were taken to establish a Canadian Navy in 1909, which was launched in 1910 in the form of two old British cruisers.

During this period there were a number of disputes to be settled with the United States, over fishing rights, boundaries and so on. Of these, the Alaska Boundary Dispute was the one which rankled most with Canadians. The dispute had a long and complex history. The Americans had a good case, but left nothing to chance, as every pressure was brought to bear to ensure that they would win at the final settlement in 1903. Canadians were bitterly disappointed, when the British representative on the Anglo-American team voted for the Americans, leaving the Yukon with no access to the Pacific.

In his pre-election tour of the West in 1910, Laurier tried to persuade the Westerners of the benefits of his new tariff agreement with the United States. This policy was rejected by the voters, who were suspicious of closer involvement with the US to the exclusion of Britain, and in 1911 Robert Borden became Prime Minister.

The automobile was slowly beginning to make an impact on Canada. In 1912 Thomas W. Wilby and F. V. Haney dipped the back wheels of their Canadian-made Reo in the waters of the Atlantic at Halifax and then drove 6,760 kilometres (4,200 miles) to Victoria where they dipped the front wheels in the Pacific waters. Over bone-jarring incomplete roads, neck-breaking stretches where roads were non-existent, through the axle-deep mud and quicksand of the prairies, on rough-hewn ferries they travelled, committed to the challenge and to the versatility of the motor-car. This was the beginning of the Canadian love affair with the car. By 1914 there were 75,000 cars in Canada, almost half of them in Ontario. Cars enabled people to visit family, meet friends and to sightsee – and they took their cameras with them.

But such simple pleasures were put aside when, on 4 August 1914, Canada entered the First World War as part of the British Empire. Soon Canadians were suffering and dying in their tens of thousands far from the sunny fields and familiar towns of home in a war that seemed endless. Photographers, sometimes anonymous, were there to record the horror of it all.

After the war, in Canada as elsewhere, things were never the same again. In the pre-war years women, along with the insane, did not have the right to vote. Now, women who had turned their hands to previously unthought-of work, including that in munitions factories, were finally all given the vote.

Soldiers, believing they had fought for a better world returned to the homes they had so innocently left, only to face the reality of unemployment and poverty. The riots during the Winnipeg General Strike were an example of a reaction that was countrywide.

Events moved along. Sir Arthur Meighen became Prime Minister for a brief period (1920–21), followed by William Lyon Mackenzie King (1921–26). In 1921 Canada's first female member of parliament was elected – Agnes MacPhail. But women's role in the workplace changed little – menial, short-term jobs, poorly paid.

By the mid-1920s Canada was fast changing from a largely agricultural nation to an urban one, and after the post-war slump there was an economic boom, reminiscent of the one of Laurier's day. These between-war years were themselves soon to be regarded with nostalgia when, in the years to follow, Canada was to experience the Depression fully and to fight in the Second World War.

The Atlantic Coast

Of Canada's four Atlantic provinces, two – Nova Scotia and New Brunswick – became part of Canada with Confederation in 1867. The third, Prince Edward Island, "the cradle of Confederation", held out until 1873. The fourth, Newfoundland, which was the first known to Europeans, was the last to join in 1949. Over the centuries events great and small had swept all over the Atlantic provinces. The explorers came and went. European fought Indian. English fought French and vice versa. Canadian fought American.

By 1895 all had settled into an economic struggle which had seldom changed and was seldom to change in the future.

It was the fish of the coastal waters and the great fishing banks off Labrador, part of Newfoundland, and the Grand Banks which had attracted the first visitors and which still provided a livelihood. And the sea and boats attracted photographers just as they attracted artists. There was always the drama of shipwrecks, of which there was never a shortage, to photograph.

At Sherbrooke, Nova Scotia, there is a an historic village which is actually part of the town. Above Cumminger Brothers general store is a tintype photography studio. This process was used in the Maritimes until 1900. Visitors can dress up in nineteenth-century costume and pose as their ancestors did all those years ago.

Fishing, mining, whaling, the seal hunt and ship-building were the mainstays of life. Just after the turn of the century attempts were made to form unions for fishermen and miners in different areas of the Atlantic provinces, in a struggle to improve the appalling conditions.

At Glace Bay, Nova Scotia, is the Cape Breton Miners' Museum, a reconstructed miner's village, complete with a miner's home of 1850 to 1900. This is one of many museums across Canada commemorating the lives of Canadians during the period these photographs cover. Where there are mines there are mining disasters, and Springhill, Nova Scotia, has had its share. In 1891, 125 men died in such a disaster, and there was a serious subterranean fire in 1916.

Almost all the work was dangerous. Even the cruel seal hunt, which for decades took as many as 15,000 men and 400 ships "to the ice" to bring back more than half a million seals, resulted in many men being killed and a large proportion of ships lost at sea.

Dr (later Sir) William Grenfell first visited Labrador in 1892 and soon set up the Grenfell Mission in an effort to alleviate the suffering of the poverty-stricken people – white, Indian and Eskimo – with hospitals, nursing stations, educational services and cottage industries.

"Monsters of the Deep, River John." This photograph depicts nature's sometimes senseless destruction. Today we know little more than these wondering residents of New Brunswick did about why sea mammals beach themselves in this way.
EDWIN CLAY BLAIR, 1918.

In the historic Maritimes, the roll-call of notable events continued. In 1901 on Newfoundland's Signal Hill, scene of a famous battle in the Seven Years' War, Guglielmo Marconi launched the era of international radio when he picked up the first wireless signal from a kite attached to a radio receiver.

Many inventions and inventors were recorded and photographed during this period, the most famous being Sir Alexander Graham Bell, who had a home during most of this period on Bras d'Or Lake in Nova Scotia. He had already invented the telephone and at Brantford, Ontario, the Bell Homestead is now a museum. There he was photographed on the day the people of Brantford unveiled their massive granite memorial to their most famous citizen. His work as a teacher of the deaf had led to his invention of the telephone. In Nova Scotia he built a tetrahedral kite, *Cygnet*, which when towed by a steamboat was able to lift a man into the air, the first time this had been done. He also built a hydrofoil craft, *HD-4*, which held the speed record for many years. He sponsored the first manned flight in Canada when the *Silver Dart* flew across Baddock Bay in 1909.

From the first airstrip built in Newfoundland at Harbour Grace, or from the later airstrip at St John's, many pioneering flights departed across the Atlantic, including those of Hawker and Grieve, Alcock and Brown, and Amelia Earhart.

In 1905 the Newfoundlander, Captain Robert (Bob) Bartlett, on one of his many Arctic expeditions, cleared from Sydney, Nova Scotia, "for the North Pole" with Peary on the SS *Roosevelt*, the only recorded time such an expedition set sail from Canada's Maritimes.

Tiny Prince Edward Island is famed as the setting for the children's story, *Anne of Green Gables*, by Lucy Maud Montgomery which she wrote there in 1908. The story was described by Mark Twain as "the sweetest creation of child life ever written".

During the First World War, Halifax, always an important port because of its ice-free harbour, became the chief eastern terminus for the Atlantic convoys organized by the Royal Navy. Business thrived as ships gathered here before joining a convoy.

At this time Halifax experienced the worst disaster ever to befall a Canadian city. On 6 December 1917 a ship full of explosives blew up in the harbour in the largest man-made explosion known before the atom bomb. More than 2,000 people were killed, 9,000 injured and many more thousands left homeless, a tragedy recorded in these photographs.

Disasters such as train wrecks, fires that engulfed churches and other important buildings – sometimes whole towns, landslides and shipwrecks provided dramatic subjects for the growing number of photographers. Even here there can sometimes be a certain charm. We see the militia, stern upholders of law and order, standing guard over what appears to our eyes to be a toy train wreck.

The greatest symbol of east-coast boat-building craftsmanship is still the *Bluenose*. Built in 1921, she was probably the fastest fishing schooner ever to have sailed the Atlantic. *Bluenose* is depicted on the Canadian ten-cent piece in recognition of her unbroken record as winner of four international schooner races. Here she leads the others in "the start of the elimination race" in 1921. Today the International Schooner Races are held annually off Lunenburg, Nova Scotia, where *Bluenose* was built.

Prohibition in the United States (1920 to 1935), which lasted longer than in Canada, provided another source of livelihood in the Maritimes, as the secluded bays were ideal for rum-running.

But the westward migration pattern of the turn-of-the-century took in the Atlantic provinces as well. Many Maritimers left, but never forgot, their rocky, watery homeland for what they hoped would be greener pastures in Ontario and the West.

Central Canada: Quebec and Ontario

Quebec and Ontario were among the four founding provinces of Confederation. At that time both were less than half the size they are today, for the boundaries were changed in 1912, each taking in a large chunk of the North.

These two provinces had the largest population and therefore benefited most from the Tariff Protection Policy which encouraged Canadian manufacturing. But town life was often just as difficult as life on the farm, and less healthy. Factories could be extremely dirty and dangerous. Hours of work were long and pay low. Women were exploited in the factories more than the men. Living conditions were often just as bad, as the basic amenities were usually far behind growth in population. Yet success seemed in the air, for by 1910 the amount of capital invested in manufacturing topped the unbelievable $1-billion mark.

Quebec was undergoing the shock of rapid transformation from an agricultural society to an urban one. Its population had increased from over a million and a half in 1901 to more than two million by 1911. A province that was two-thirds rural in 1891 was by 1911 half urban.

In 1908 the Quebec tercentenary had been commemorated with great ceremony and extravagant celebrations, including pageants with a cast of 5,000, beautifully costumed, who acted out historic moments with the magnificent St Lawrence as a backdrop. The pageants are recorded in marvellous long concertina-type photographs which fold out, of which a detail from one is shown here.

French-Canadians were determined to press for the duality of race and language guaranteed by equality before the law. The execution of Louis Riel in 1885 had been taken as a direct affront by the province, and the Manitoba Schools Question roused much debate over French language rights. There was a particular concern to avoid foreign wars, and any involvement in the South African War was strongly opposed by French-Canadian politicians. Compulsory conscription during the First World War was even more strenuously opposed, both before and after it became law.

Although Laurier had side-stepped direct government involvement in the South African War, his fellow French-Canadians still considered him to be too pro-English and too willing to compromise. From 1907 Henri Bourassa led a campaign against Laurier's liberalism, in the process founding *Le Devoir* in 1910. Laurier was rejected by French Canada in the election of 1911.

French-Canadians also took part in the westward migration pattern, tens of thousands moving into eastern and northern Ontario to work in the lumber camps and in the mines. Most were unwilling to endure hard winters and the short growing season of the West itself.

English-speaking Canadians were venturing farther afield, often to Quebec, where they happily photographed the quaint stone houses, picturesque villages, roadside shrines and wintry scenes.

In 1904 the Montreal Ski Club was formed and the next year organized its first excursion to the Laurentians, which had been declared a park by the Quebec government in 1895. The first ski school was set up in 1911 and by the 1920s the trend towards this immensely popular sport had begun. There are a number of sporting activities recorded in the collection, some of which – hockey, lacrosse, football and curling – are shown here.

To help promote immigration, photographs were taken of whole families safely arrived at the Quebec Immigration Centre. These photographs were then sent back to the immigrant's former country to encourage and reassure others.

There are photographs of new buildings being opened, and new bridges being built, like the Quebec Bridge, which was opened in 1917 as North America's greatest cantilever bridge.

To our eyes there is a neatness about most of the photographs, especially of new buildings. But not neat enough, apparently. On some photographs in the collection lawns – even people – are carefully painted in.

In other photographs, cut-out people are placed in a painted setting. There are a number of composite photographs in the collection – head-and-shoulders photographs of individuals put together to form one all-encompassing photograph.

During this period many boundary lines were being drawn-up or re-set, a job made easier by the use of the camera.

In Ontario, The Ontario Hydro-Electric Power Commission had been formed in 1906, making use of the enormous power of Niagara Falls, itself one of the most renowned and earliest subjects for photographers in North America. In the 1850s the Langenheim brothers of Philadelphia were famous for a series of panoramic views of Niagara Falls, one which was presented to Louis Jacques Mandé Daguerre, inventor of the Daguerrotype, who was full of praise. (Daguerre himself was the first person to publicly announce, in Paris in 1839, that he had succeeded in fixing an image on a plate using a camera obscura.)

The Toronto merchandising empires of the T. Eaton Company (1868) and its rival Simpsons (1871) were well founded and thriving. Toronto, like Montreal, was burgeoning and becoming more cosmopolitan. The two cities were rivals for the title of "the leading city of Canada". Other cities like Ottawa were proudly photographing their growing skylines.

The fruit farms of the Niagara Peninsula were being laid out. Wheat was grown initially, but the warmer climate of the strip of land between the Niagara Escarpment and Lake Ontario was more usefully exploited when farmers switched to planting peach and cherry trees. The Peninsula is one of the very few areas in Canada where these tender fruits can be grown.

The 1920s were a time of artistic regeneration. The artists who formed the Group of Seven painted Canadian landscapes in a raw and rugged way, which was inspired by the land itself. They travelled all over Canada, but their most famous paintings are of Northern Ontario and Quebec. Photographers were also visiting these remote places, which at that time few Canadians had seen, and recorded the beauty of the land with their cameras. As early as 1888 the Toronto Amateur Photographic Association had been formed, in 1891 renamed the Toronto Camera Club, one of many new clubs and societies across the country devoted to this new art.

The West

"The West" had been wholly owned by the Hudson Bay Company until 1870 when it was purchased by the Canadian government, and in 1873 the Province of Manitoba was formed in a tiny square within it. By

1895 the West was officially part of the Northwest Territories, the Government of Canada taking action to ward off the acquisitive glances of the United States. But now it was a place where the Indians no longer hunted the countless buffalo as they had done since time immemorial. For Canada had, since 1886, been made one by the transcontinental railway. And with the railway came the first flow of hunters, sightseers and settlers who indiscriminately shot the buffalo, often from the moving trains, until, unbelievably, these magnificent animals were soon on the verge of extinction.

Once the flow of settlers began, it rapidly turned into a torrent, with the encouragement, promotion and help of the Canadian government. Clifford Sifton, Canada's Minister of the Interior from 1896 to 1905, had decided that the West must be settled quickly to keep the West for Canada. Until this time many American politicians thought it was a foregone conclusion that the United States would take over this vast area.

Sifton knew exactly the type of settler he wanted: "a peasant in a sheepskin coat . . . with a stout wife and half a dozen children". He realized that it was essential to have experienced farmers from Britain and Europe. Hundreds of thousands responded to the government advertising campaigns in their own lands, which included colourful posters showing a prosperous wheat farm and extolling: "Wheat land. Rich virgin soil. Land for mixed farming. This is your opportunity. Why not embrace it?" There were photographs of the prairies and of settlers who had arrived. Photographs in the collection show settlers from Ruthenia, Galicia, Austria, Russia and elsewhere. They are posed by their sod huts or tilling the grass-covered plains that had never before been turned.

The government was making an irresistible offer: 65 hectares (160 acres) per man, free after he had developed it over three years and had become a British subject. A further 160 acres was available to each man over eighteen. Scottish tenant farmers, eager for land of their own, were judged by Sifton to be the "best settlers in the world".

The land was there, it was free and the price of wheat was to increase by thirty-five per cent in the British market between 1896 and 1913.

But there was another, even greater attraction for many – religious freedom. A number of religious sects, like the Doukhobors, 7,500 of whom came to Canada from Russia in 1899, were willing to endure any hardship if this freedom were guaranteed. There are photographs of Doukhobors in this collection. They left Russia because they had been persecuted for their religious beliefs, which included refusing to go to war and refusing to send their children to school. All was

not necessarily smooth in the new land on these issues, and their unique form of protest was to strip naked, much to the bewilderment of Victorian officialdom.

Between 1891 and 1901 the population of the West, albeit over a vast area, increased by sixty-six per cent. By 1900 the foreign-born people of the West formed more than twenty-seven per cent of the population. The new settlers had a number of daunting problems to overcome. First, they had to actually find the land they had been assigned, not an easy task on the then largely trackless prairies. They had to build a home – often a sod hut for the first few years, their only protection from the cruelly cold winters, provide for their families, learn a new language and customs, and contend with the great extremes of the elements. There are photographs of the Land Registry Office in Moose Jaw and of homesteaders trekking to their land.

Although Manitoba became a province in 1870, it was enlarged in 1905 (and 1949) and in 1905 the provinces of Saskatchewan and Alberta were created. There is a photograph showing "the very moment" Alberta became a province with great ceremony and celebration. Alberta's population was 73,000 in 1901. By 1911 it had become 375,000.

In Saskatchewan alone, which had received 450,000 newcomers between 1885 and 1910, there were distinct settlements of British, Dutch, French, German, Hungarian, Doukhobor, Temperance, Hutterite, Mennonite, US Negro, Ukrainian, Scandinavian, Polish and Jewish. There were also, of course, thousands of individuals and families from these and other countries, including the Austro-Hungarian Empire, Italy and China.

Even within this vast array there were peculiarities like the Isaac Barr colony. In 1903 Moses Isaac Barr took almost 2,000 English men, women and children to Canada "to keep Canada for the British". Most were totally unprepared, having come from banks and shops, and did their chores, so it was said, in spats and bowlers. In one of the more colourful episodes in Canadian land-settlement history, the colonists, after many disappointments and hardships, deposed their leader who they considered to be incompetent and a charlatan. This episode ended in heartbreak for many and Barr disappeared, but the site of their settlement is now Lloydminster.

Even the Salvation Army was involved, urging the mass migration to Canada of an over-abundance of English widows.

A powerful farming organization was quickly formed, and when, in the summer of 1910, Laurier made his whistle-stop pre-election tour of the West, intended to be a triumphal progress, he was met along the way by organized groups of farmers with a formidable list of complaints and demands, from tariff reciprocity with the US to an increase in Btitish preference.

Meanwhile, National Parks had been created, such as Waterton Lakes National Park in 1895 and Jasper in 1907. Banff, the first, had been formed in 1885, and has now celebrated its centennial. As early as 1903 Banff had its own Natural History Museum. Photographs of the prairies and especially' the spectacular mountain chains on Canada's West Coast were fascinating to the people back East. There are photographs of Writing-on-Stone Park and Twin Falls Valley in Yoho. The magnificent falls there had only just been discovered. In 1906 Elk Island National Park was formed in northern Alberta as a preserve for the elk, and in 1922 Wood Buffalo National Park was established astride the northern Albertan and Northwest Territories' border. The foresight on the part of the government of Canada in setting up these enormous parks so early in its history, seems extraordinary in the light of all the problems such a young country had to face.

In the West, as elsewhere, progress was rapid. As early as 1906 Winnipeg had a public telephone system. Important buildings were being erected, like Alberta's Legislative Building in Edmonton, built between 1907 and 1912.

The West, too, had its share of disasters. One of the most famous was the Frank Slide of 1903 when over eighty-one million tonnes (eighty million tons) of rock crashed down Turtle Mountain on to the town of Frank. At least seventy-five lives were lost.

By 1895 the Indians of the West had been pushed on to reserves, reserves that were far too small for survival by their traditional means – which they were not encouraged to pursue in any case. At this time in the reign of Queen Victoria, the myth of the "Noble Savage" persisted. The true nobility of the red man was not acceptable, whereas a romanticized version was.

It was thought best, and most convenient for the white man, for Indians to live in small pious communities where they could be protected from themselves and white men. Between the years 1871 and 1877 seven treaties had been signed, giving the government the southern part of the prairie provinces. The Indian Act of 1880 sealed the doom of these native peoples. The large-scale help promised the Indians, for "as long as the sun shall shine", never materialized. One result was the Riel Rebellion in 1885 when Louis Riel encouraged Indians and Métis (people of Indian and European blood) to demand fulfilment of their treaty rights.

The treaties and the reserve system transformed the Indians overnight from free hunters and providers into dependent prisoners on their own land. Celebrations such as the Sun Dance were banned, and Indian children were sent to boarding schools, often run by the church, for nine or ten months of the year.

Some Indians resisted. As early as 1900 a number of British Columbia bands had organized themselves to fight in the courts for recognition of their land claims, and there were a few similar efforts elsewhere in Canada. Attempts to form Indian associations in the 1920s and 1930s failed. The Indians were suspicious and the government discouraged the idea.

Many years were to pass before such attempts were again made to reverse the trend of what usually was toward extreme deprivation.

There are a number of fine photographs of Indians taken during this period. Some were still willing to pose in their head-dresses and garments to have their photographs taken, sometimes with famous individuals or with the Royal Canadian Mounted Police. Some photographs were taken at fairs, where the Indians were probably "appearing". Other photographs were taken at their own celebrations, and some in a more truthful setting. There are hints of the past, for example "raising the pole of the sun dance tent". Often the expressions on their faces sum up their lives and future in a way that words could not.

The Pacific Coast

British Columbia had become a province in 1871 on the promise that a railway would be built linking it with the rest of Canada. The story of the construction of the Canadian Pacific Railway is among the most enthralling in Canadian history. The problems to be overcome in the water and rock north of Lake Superior, and in the passes of the Rockies and other mountain ranges, remain as remarkable a feat today as they were when the last spike was driven in, late in 1885, and the first train crossed Canada in 1886.

There are photographs of summer festivities, always an important feature of the hot Canadian summers, so we have the beach at Kelowna, BC, with ladies in their Edwardian finery viewing the acquatic activities.

As early as 1800 the Okanagan Valley was famed for its fruit-growing, and in one photograph the neat rows of trees somehow complement the beautiful setting. From the beginning, British Columbia had attracted gentlemen farmers. Even today, Victoria is considered to be more English than England.

In the pre-First World War years some of the young gentlemen launched farming and irrigation projects in a barren interior part of BC. When war was declared, they left their tools; most of them never returned.

Stanley Park in Vancouver had been formed in 1889 as a woodland park when there were great forests

"Presenting the Calumet to the Great Spirit by Chief Skeet"
near Thunder Bay, Ontario.
WILLIAM S. PIPER, 1920.

everywhere. From the park's earliest days notables such as Governor-General Lord Grey and his party posed in front of the park's Old Hollow Tree, just as tourists do today. In 1893 the then Governor-General, Lord Stanley, after whom the park was named, made another important contribution to Canadian life – he donated hockey's Stanley Cup.

But there had been problems too. In 1907 there was rioting against the large Asiatic community and from then on a gentleman's agreement existed between the governments of Canada and Japan limiting the number of immigrants. The Chinese had, of course, made a major contribution in labour to the construction of the trans-Canada railway. There were disasters too when, in 1910, sixty-two railway workers were killed in an avalanche in Rogers' Pass and, in 1915, fifty-seven men were killed in an avalanche of snow and mud at a mining camp.

Another chapter was added to the story of Canada's railways when in 1916 the Rogers' Pass tunnel was opened. Called the Connaught Tunnel, it went through Mount Macdonald in the Selkirk range rather than over it as the previous line had done. The eight-kilometre (five-mile) long tunnel, allowed thirty-five kilometres (twenty-two miles) of the original avalanche-prone line over the summit to be abandoned.

The North

The discovery of gold in the Yukon was one of the most dramatic occurrences in Canada within the period covered by these photographs. In 1895, in anticipation of a gold rush, the Yukon was made a territory, and a detachment of the North-West Mounted Police (to become the Royal Canadian Mounted Police) was despatched to maintain law and order.

Gold was duly discovered in 1896 and thousands of men and women from around the world set off for the Klondike. There are photographs of the queue for a miner's license at Victoria, of boats leaving Victoria, packed with would-be miners, for Skagway Bay, of Dawson itself and the struggles to haul in equipment. Stories of the climb over the Chilkoot Pass and of the colourful local characters have become legend.

When the gold ran out, the population dropped dramatically – from more than 30,000 people at the peak of the Gold Rush to 4,157 in 1921 and stagnation quickly set in.

The British had ceded the Arctic islands of the Northwest Territories to Canada in 1880. Very few people had seen Canada's North, and few wanted to see it or even thought about it. However, polar exploration continued. In the collection there are photographs of Roald Amundsen, the great Norwegian, who successfully negotiated the Northwest Passage in the years 1903 to 1906 in the converted herring-boat *Gjøa*. Amundsen shared with Peary qualities of determination and high organization which meant that they succeeded where others failed.

Steffanson's expedition (1913 to 1918) in the *Karluk* cleared from Victoria. While Steffanson was on a hunting expedition, the boat drifted and was eventually crushed and sank before the expedition had properly begun. The crew and scientists then hiked across the pack ice for ninety-six kilometres (sixty miles) to Wrangel Island, north of Russia and claimed it for Britain. Captain Robert Bartlett set off with one Eskimo and a dog-sled on a 1,125-kilometre (700-mile) journey to Siberia for help. The Russians re-claimed the island by force in 1924. The Arctic islands prompted many expeditions to affirm ownership during these and the following years.

Knud Rasmussen in 1923 traversed the Northwest Passage overland. In the collection there are photographs of the Inuit (Eskimos), on whose help the explorers often depended when their ships were crushed in the ice or some other disaster occurred.

Canada and the First World War

When the First World War was declared on 4 August 1914, Canadians were eager to defend the motherland. Many had recently arrived from Britain, and the glories of the Empire, Queen Victoria's Jubilees and the South African War were fresh in the public consciousness.

In August 1914 Canada had a "standing army" of only 3,110 men. Within two months of the outbreak of war 30,000 men were armed and sent to Britain in a convoy of thirty-two ships. The Great War is the single most important event to be covered by the photographs in this collection.

In 1914 the photographs reflect great patriotism. There are mascots – often a bulldog – posed with the Union Jack. The dog might have a money box strapped to its back to collect funds for the war effort, or there might simply be a message, such as "Waiting for the call." There are innumerable photographs of fresh-faced young men posed proudly, singly or together, in immaculate uniforms, and of military training camps. Then there are the embarkation scenes, at railway stations or harbours on both coasts. By 1916 there is a posed "Mother of Sorrow" figure and soon a number of war memorials for village, town and city make their appearance.

But this was in the future. When the Canadians arrived in England they were disappointed to find that they had to spend the winter in uncomfortable camps on Salisbury Plain, where they were eventually reviewed by King George V. On their arrival in England, Lord Kitchener, British Minister of War, had not been impressed with their level of training and decided to split them up among British divisions. This idea was fiercely and successfully resisted by Colonel Sam Hughes. Sam Hughes, a larger than life figure, was Canada's Minister of Defense and Militia. He had, through the strength of his own personality, been responsible for recruiting a large number of the volunteers. The Canadians stayed together.

Although one Canadian detachment, the Princess Patricia's Light Infantry, had reached France by Christmas of 1914, the Canadian division itself crossed to France in February 1915.

They and the 400,000 Canadians who followed distinguished themselves in the nightmares of Ypres, Loos, Passchendaele and the Battle of the Somme. In the latter, to give but one example of the wholesale slaughter which prevailed throughout, of the 753 soldiers of the Newfoundland Regiment, all but sixty-eight were either killed or wounded.

The capture of Vimy Ridge was the most significant achievement of the Canadian Army in the First World War. British Columbians and Nova Scotians, French Canadians and prairie farmers planned and carried out an important breakthrough on the western front. This was the first time that the Canadians, by now numbering four divisions, had been united as one fighting unit. This was the stuff of legends.

By June 1917 the Canadians finally had a Canadian Corps Commander – Sir Arthur Currie – a competent Commander, who prior to the war had, rather surprisingly, been a real-estate agent.

By the end of the war nearly 25,000 Canadians had served with the Royal Naval Air Service, the Royal Flying Corps and the Royal Air Force. Canada's "Billy" Bishop was the most famous wartime pilot with seventy-two victories. All of this led to the formation of the Royal Canadian Air Force in 1924.

When the First World War ended on 11 November 1918, more than 600,000 men and women had served in the Canadian Expeditionary Force. Of these 173,000 were wounded and 60,000 never returned.

With reason, it could be said that the camera, primitive tool that it was compared with today's sophisticated pieces of apparatus, recorded the maturing of a great nation. It recorded the vicissitudes of its people and those fleeting moments of real historic importance, though these, in retrospect, may perhaps be considered less important than the simple everyday chronicling of events which is captured so engagingly in these pages. Canada and the world of photography had come of age together.

THE PHOTOGRAPHS

"John Baran's House."
HOWARD HENRY ALLEN, 1913.

"Twin Falls, Yoho Valley, BC."
The twin falls of Yoho's Takakkaw Falls make it the highest of
Canada's numerous spectacular waterfalls. The water from
Daly Glacier falls a total of 503 metres (1650 feet).
Suprisingly the falls were first seen by a white man as late as the 1880s,
and photographs were sent back for the fascinated Easterners to view.
To the Cree Indians it had always been Takakkaw –
"magnificent".
WILLIAM NOTMAN AND SONS, 1902.

WILD
SPLENDOUR

When the first train crossed Canada early in 1886, "the wonderland of Canada" was made accessible to the people back East. A publication of 1908 proclaimed: "The Alps would be lost to view in this great assemblage of sky-piercing summits, these vast ramparts and domes and turrets". Canadians soon claimed that the Rockies and other mountain ranges were better than fifty Switzerlands. Swiss guides were, however, engaged to work at Banff, Canada's first national park.

"Ice cave Illecillewaet Glacier." A beautifully dramatic stereoscopic photograph of an ice cave in this glacier in the Selkirk Mountains, now within Glacier National Park, BC. The ice field drops 1,097 metres (3,600 feet) into the valley. From its foot the Illecillewaet River flows to the mighty Columbia. When three-dimensional stereoscopic photography was first introduced, it was considered to be "The Optical Wonder of the Age."
BYRON HARMON, 1908.

ABOVE

"Writing-on-Stone." These early settlers are
insignificant, placed as they are in this setting
against hoodos – strange rock formations – of
Writing-on-Stone Provincial Park in the badlands of
Alberta. The name of the park comes from the
petroglyphs (carvings on stone) and pictographs
(rock paintings) done by the Indians on the cliffs
along the Milk River.

A. RAFTON-CANNING, 1910.

RIGHT

"Capilano Valley and The Lions, Vancouver, B.C."
The Lions, seen in the distance, are the twin peaks
that "guard" Vancouver.

ROBERT GEORGE LAMB, 1920.

Windsor Public Library

"Kennedy Lake".
WALTER M. DRAYCOTT, 1923.

"Goat Mountain from the Summit of Crown Mountain. Crow's Nest Pass, BC." This area was opened up with the coming of the railway. Crow's Nest Pass is one of only three passes through the formidable mountains. This is the most southern of the three, and at its highest is 1,356 metres (4,450 feet). The area of the pass extends for forty-five kilometres (twenty-eight miles) between Lundbreck, BC and the British Columbia boundary. From 1897 to 1983 there was a special cheap rate – known as the Crow Rate – for shipping grain through the pass, agreed by the federal government and the Canadian Pacific Railway. The natural beauty and the role of the pass in linking Canada has led to its being declared an area of national historic significance.
JOSEPH FRED SPALDING, 1908.

"South Kanaka Creek Falls, Webster's Corners, BC."
WILLIAM JAY VAN "PT", 1915.

"Go Home River", near Georgian Bay in Ontario. John Witherspoon Bald (1867–1961) recorded many facets of life in his home communities Penetanguishene (from 1898 to 1900) and Midland, Ontario (from 1900 to 1955), and, as here, in the surrounding area of woods and water.

JOHN WITHERSPOON BALD, 1907.

"Niagara Falls. No. 1." One of a series of contact prints of the Falls, one of the earliest and probably the most favourite subject for photographers. By the time this photograph was taken, Niagara Falls – the American Falls and the Canadian Horseshoe Falls – had been photographed for more than fifty years. As early as 1860 William Notman, Canada's famous early photographer, was advertising one hundred stereoscopic views of Niagara. Sightseers preferred to appear in a photograph with the Falls as a backdrop. If this could not be arranged, a painted backdrop was sometimes used.
PANORAMIC CAMERA COMPANY OF CANADA, 1913.

"Quebec Ice Bridge." During very severe winters the St Lawrence River at Quebec City freezes solid – as does the Niagara River just below the falls – and a natural bridge is formed across the river. The winter of 1909 to 1910 provided such a subject for photographs.
ALFRED DUPRÉ, 1910.

"A storm in St. Mary's Bay", Nova Scotia.
WILLIAM PLAYLE, 1914.

"Percé Rock." Visitors to the Gaspé Peninsula have always marvelled at Rocher Percé, here viewed from the south. It has seen much of Canada's history pass by. In 1534 Jacques Cartier sheltered his fleet behind this great, somewhat ship-like, monolith.
DOLOR N. CADORET, 1919.

In "Captive Lynx", the trapped lynx stops snarling to look at the man with the gun moments before the shot is fired. In the next photograph in this series of three, the photographer, a woman, has apparently handed the camera to the hunter while she holds up the lifeless, and surprisingly not very large, animal by its hind legs to be photographed.

LUCY MARGARET FORBES, 1921.

The wealth of deer and other wildlife in the forested, watery Lake-of-the-Woods area in Ontario, near the Manitoba border, has for many years attracted hunters. Here they have arranged "the kill" with an attempt at artistry.

C. G. LINDE, 1913.

THE GREAT COLDNESS

"Group of Eskimo women and children at Fullerton, 1906." These Inuit, as Eskimo people now prefer to be called, were photographed by Geraldine Moodie, who is renowned for her fine photographs of Indians and Eskimos. Her husband, also a keen amateur photographer, was a Royal North West Mounted Police officer, and she often accompanied him on trips to Indian settlements and to the Arctic. When they travelled by ship, she sometimes set up a studio on board, and invited the Inuit to have their photographs taken.
GERALDINE MOODIE, 1907.

LEFT
An Inuit man, one of several native men and women photographed by Flaherty. It was said of Flaherty that he "found in the Eskimo a humanity so golden that he carried it with him ever afterward as a touchstone of judgement".
ROBERT J. FLAHERTY, 1911

"Crawford Tram Co, of Nelson, BC taking one and one eighth inch
cable to the Silver Dollar Mine. Length of cable 3,600 feet. Weight
of cable 7,600 lb. Packed by E. J. Brantford and Co Camborne, BC
on 31 horses, distance six miles up the mountain trail on Oct. 3,
1906."
E. T. TUCKER, 1906.

ABOVE RIGHT
"Klondikers buying Miner's Licenses at Custom House, Victoria,
BC." Gold fever on a cold February day.
I. M. JONES, 1898.

BELOW RIGHT
"Winter Scene in Miles Canyon".
E. J. HAMACHER, 1902

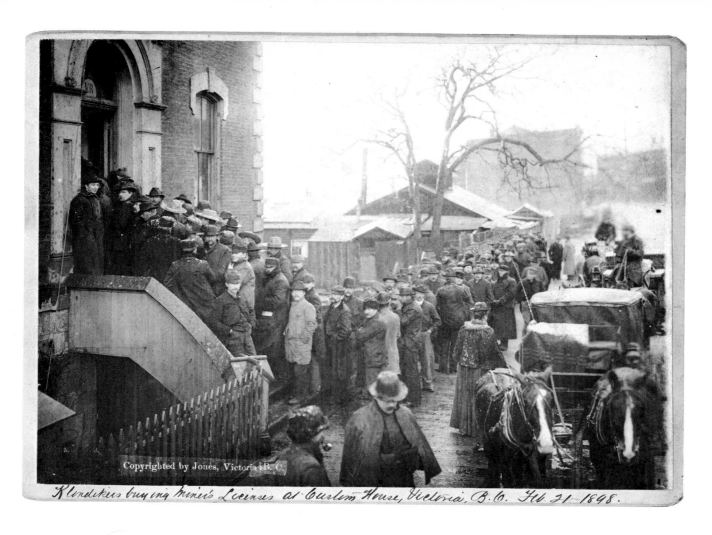

Copyrighted by Jones, Victoria, B. C.

Klondikers buying miner's Licenses at Custom House, Victoria, B.C. Feb 21-1898.

WINTER SCENE IN MILES CANYON
COPYRIGHTED BY E. J. HAMACHER
WHITE HORSE, Y.T. APRIL 7, 1902
#1102

CAPTAIN RAOUL AMUNDSEN,
DISCOVERER OF NORTH WEST PASSAGE.

"Captain Roald Amundsen, Discoverer of North West Passage." Roald Amundsen, a Norwegian, was the first man to navigate the Northwest Passage. In his converted fishing boat, *Gjøa*, he found his way between the mainland and the Arctic islands between 1903 and 1906. The sea route from the Atlantic to the Pacific, after centuries of dreams and attempts, had finally been found. Amundsen's success was probably due to his careful planning and great determination. In December of 1911 he beat Scott to the South Pole by one month.

JOHN FRANCIS SUCRE, 1906.

"Hauling spud weighing 27 tons to Bear Creek for the Canadian Klondike Mining Co's dredge, the largest in the world." An event in the Klondike – the arrival of a giant spud, or drilling piece – also gives us a rare view of main street and the Nugget Saloon of Bear Creek, a settlement a few kilometres from Dawson.

ERLING OLAV ELLINGSEN, 1910.

"R.N.W.M. Police Barracks and Churchill River, Churchill, 1907." A Hudson's Bay Company fur trading post was set up near here as early as 1685. The town was named for the governor of the Company, John Churchill, who later became Duke of Marlborough.

The North West Mounted Police had been created in 1873. Their presence in Canada's North and West led to a peaceful settlement in those vast areas. In 1904 they became the Royal North West Mounted Police, and in 1920 the Royal Canadian Mounted Police.

GERALDINE MOODIE, 1907.

"R.N.W.M.P. Patrol Dawson to Herschel Island Dec. the 27 1908."
This was an expedition of some 644 kilometres (400 miles) to
Herschel Island in Mackenzie Bay. The Mounties had a base on
Herschel Island, which was of great importance to Arctic explorers.
JERRY DOODY, 1909.

RIGHT
Two Eskimos and an Indian from Robert Flaherty's
album.
ROBERT J. FLAHERTY, 1911

A selection of photographs from an album entitled "Through Canada's North Land". It is very much like any family album of the time, except that it records an Arctic expedition of 1911. The photographs by Robert J. Flaherty are seldom seen views of the Inuit (Eskimos), the northern Cree Indians and life in the North, before this way of life vanished. Flaherty, an iron-ore prospector, made four geological expeditions to the Hudson Bay and Ungava regions between 1910 and 1915. He was the first white man to cross Ungava by dog team. As a result of these experiences he wrote several books and later made the famous film, *Nanook of the North*, a valuable social documentary on the Inuit.
ROBERT J. FLAHERTY, 1911.

Brotherly Love Cottage. A sense of humour was essential for survival in the extreme climate and unrelenting isolation.

Supplies are transferred from the expedition ship.

A member of the expedition posing
with a quartet of shy little girls.

A waterfall rages in Ungava, as the
snow melts.

The buildings of the white community.

A woman, possibly of mixed blood, perched on some of the supplies delivered by the expedition ship, which can be seen in the background.

A memorable photograph of Inuit people in church. Various churches competed for converts in the Arctic, and soon exercised considerable power. Inuit children were often taken away from their parents and sent to church boarding schools for nine or ten months of the year. But the missionaries were usually the only ones interested in an already distressed people.

Teepees of the northern Cree.

LEFT
An Inuit man in school with a map of the world to
contemplate. The writing on the blackboard is in
the Eskimo language, written in the alphabet the
missionaries devised for them.

This family arranged itself round its youngest member
for the photographer.

LEFT
The streams and rivers of the North provided
a bountiful supply of fish for the native people.

Tom Threepersons
Champion Bronco Bus

THE LAST, BEST WEST

Swenson Macleod alta.

of the world.

Detail from "Topping a Bad One." Breaking a wild horse was but one subject in a series of photographs depicting the wild west. Western Canada Ranching Series No. 14.

A. E. BROWN, 1912.

LEFT

"Tom Threepersons, Champion Bronco Buster of the world" at McLeod, Alberta. There were, predictably, similar claims by others, all part of the spirit and colour of the West.

JENS E. SWENSON, 1912.

45

"Pioneer." We can never know what persuaded this
lady to ride side-saddle on a steer, or, for that
matter, what persuaded the steer to allow itself to be
saddled and bridled.
CHRIS J. KNUDSON, 1910.

"Last of the Canadian Buffaloes." The few remnants of Canada's once immense, indeed countless, numbers
of buffalo were by this time protected in national and provincial parks. As white men replaced the Indians,
so white men's cattle took the place of the buffalo – on which the Prairie Indians had almost totally depended.
STEELE & CO., 1902.

The odd, somewhat grotesque, form of the prickly-pear was a worthy subject for Geraldine Moodie, most famous for her later photographs of native peoples. Prairie flora, like the prickly-pear with its showy lemon-yellow flowers and barbed bristles – somewhat difficult to remove from the skin, are very much part of the prairie scene. This photographer made several studies of prairie flowers at Maple Creek, Saskatchewan.

GERALDINE MOODIE, 1898.

"Lieut. Sousa and Indians." John Philip Sousa, famous bandmaster and composer of marches, toured many countries with his band. He was appearing at Brandon, Manitoba when he met these Plains Indians.

HOWARD HENRY ALLEN, 1919.

"Blood Indian Pow-Wow Dance." These Plains Indians sometimes dressed up to perform dances and ceremonies at fairs. And on occasion, as here near Lethbridge, Alberta, there was the feeling that the past was very close.

THE BRITISH AND COLONIAL PHOTOGRAPHIC CO, 1910.

"Blood Indian Squaws, Papooses, Ponies and Travois, Macleod, Alberta." A harsher view of what life was really like.

A. RAFTON-CANNING, 1910.

"Raising the centre pole, sundance tent." The Sun Dance had been banned for some time, along with all other celebrations, ceremonies and rituals.
GERALDINE MOODIE, 1899.

"Squaw Dance, Blackfoot Indians, Macleod, Alberta."
The chiefs sit apart to view the dance.
THE CONSOLIDATED STATIONERY CO., LTD., 1907.

"Homestead Rush Land Office, Moose Jaw." The rush for free land in Saskatchewan was equalled
elsewhere on the Canadian prairie – advertised as "the last, best west."
LEWIS RICE, 1909.

"Homesteaders trekking from Moose Jaw, Saskatchewan." A home could be built from
sod, but it was essential to take the stovepipes with you.
LEWIS RICE, 1909.

"Interior of Ruthenian home, Alberta." A rare interior view, showing the baby in its basket hanging safely from the ceiling. The etching on the wall may be of Leo Tolstoy.
MIRIAM ELSTOR, 1911.

"Ruthenian settlers, Alberta." The homestead established and a house built, this family can relax to smile and laugh for the photographer.
MIRIAM ELSTOR, 1911.

"The Autumn Hunter" photographed near Maple Creek, Saskatchewan. A painted backdrop has been used by the photographer to enhance an already splendid outfit of this Plains Cree Indian.
G. E. FLEMING, 1907.

"An Autumn Outing" near Edmonton, Alberta. A lady rides side-saddle on her fine mount, photographed in the same year as the warrior opposite.

CASSEL M. KATE, 1907.

Peter Verigin Photo by E. J. Campbell
COPY DEPOSITED NO. 39862

Peter Verigin was the leader of the Doukhobors, who had settled around Yorkton. When he arrived from Russia in 1903, 1,600 Doukhobors trekked to Winnipeg to meet him. Over the years 1908 to 1912, he led the more militant Doukhobors, "The Sons of Freedom", to Grand Forks, British Columbia. Verigin died near Grand Forks when a time bomb blew up in the railway carriage in which he was travelling.

E. J. CAMPBELL, 1922.

The Doukhobor Pilgrims Entering Yorkton

"The Doukhobor Pilgrims Entering Yorkton." The first Doukhobors, a religious sect from Russia, arrived in Yorkton, Saskatchewan in 1899, sponsored by Leo Tolstoy and the English Quakers. They were drawn to Canada from Tsarist Russia by the promise of religious freedom. Their beliefs included pacificism and not sending their children to school. When thwarted, their form of non-violent protest was to strip naked, much to the consternation of Victorian Canadian officialdom. Another photograph taken at the same time is entitled "Doukhobor Pilgrims Refusing To Go Back To Their Village". Although we do not know the exact circumstances, they did, on this occasion, remain clothed.

THOMAS VEITCH SIMPSON, 1902.

"Edmonton – This very moment is THE CAPITAL & ALBERTA A Province in Reality."
1 September 1905 was an emotional day for those who had worked so hard to make their homes here.
Present were the Prime Minister, Sir Wilfred Laurier (left), and the Governor-General, Lord Grey (seated).
Most fittingly, an impressive contingent of Royal North West Mounted Police added colour and authority
to the occasion. The Mounties were part of the story of the West.

GEORGE D. CLARK, 1905.

The Province of Saskatchewan was also created in 1905, and the first Legislature met in 1906, commemorated
in this composite photograph. The Mace – symbol of office and authority – has pride of place.
And the young page has not been left out. Walter Scott gave up his position as
Publisher and Editor of the *Regina Leader* to become the first Premier.

EDGAR C. ROSSIE PHOTOS, 1906.

55

PEOPLE

"His First Air Ship." An idealized view of childhood, typical of the period. Mention of air ships and airplanes was by now creeping into everyday language.
EDWARD ADOLPHUS PRICE, 1915.

LEFT
"Pear Blossoms in Mr Stirling's orchard, Kelowna, BC."
G. H. E. HUDSON, 1909.

"I.O.D.E. Rose Ball." Members of the Independent Order of the Daughters of the Empire have since 1900 striven to preserve the British heritage in Canada and have done much good work for charity. Social occasions were important. This wintry February evening in Toronto was brightened by the Rose Ball held at the elegant King Edward Hotel. The Lieutenant-Governor of Ontario and his wife attended.

F. W. MICKLETHWAITE, 1911.

ABOVE RIGHT

On the political front, Sir Wilfred Laurier had been Prime Minister from 1893 to 1911, a period of economic boom. But it was time for a change. His 1910 pre-election tour of the West was intended to be a triumphal progress. In the event, he was met by groups with petitions and complaints at almost every stop. Here at Mission City, BC in August 1910, he met a local representative.

WILLIAM T. COOKSLEY, 1910.

BELOW RIGHT

Sir Wilfred Laurier at a night-time rally in Montreal on 27 September 1916. The platform is decorated with flags and dramatically large plaques of Laurier. The few ladies present are in the bedecked galleries.

MONTREAL STANDARD PUBLISHING COMPANY LIMITED, 1916.

"Before the Evening Service".
J. ANDISON COCKBURN, 1899.

ABOVE RIGHT
Mug shots from the Identification Department of the Calgary Police Force. Most offences were
vagrancy, drinking, gambling or theft.

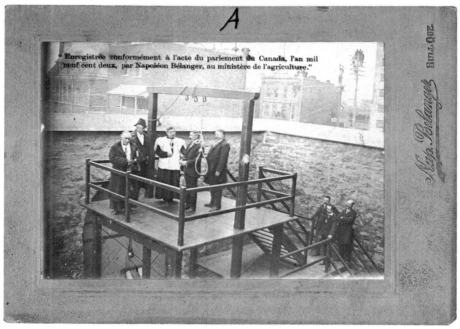

"Execution of Lacroix at Hull, Quebec on 21 July 1902." One of a pair of photographs depicting this event. In the next the hood has been placed over his head. Lacroix is holding a rosary which has been carefully touched up in the photograph, so it won't be missed.

NAPOLÉON BELANGER, 1902.

"Lord Strathcona." Donald Alexander Smith was created 1st Baron Strathcona and Mount Royal to acknowledge his services to Canada. By 1908 the grand old man had seen much of Canada's history – indeed, been part of it. He started as an administrator for the Hudson's Bay Company, became a member of Parliament, and was sent West to negotiate with Riel. His most notable achievements were, with his cousin George Stephen, completing the greater part of the Great Northern Railway and then the Canadian Pacific Railway. In 1885 it was Donald Smith who drove in the last spike.

In 1861 Notman had been appointed photographer to the Queen. As such his studio was the obvious choice for important Canadians and visiting dignitaries.

WILLIAM NOTMAN AND SON, 1908.

"John Salda", a Stoney Indian.
BYRON HARMON, 1907.

"St Joseph's Academy Alumnae Banquet, Toronto, 29 October 1911." The waitresses
paused in the serving of the soup course so this photograph could be taken.
F. W. MICKLETHWAITE, 1911.

ABOVE LEFT

"Miss Helen Taft at Burlington during the Quebec Tercentenary Celebrations." An
Indian encampment was set up beside the open-air stage where the celebrations and
pageants took place in 1908. The Indians – fringed, feathered, beaded, and clean – posed
with visiting dignitaries, such as the daughter of the new President of the United States.
They also took part in the pageants. The photographer's stamp on this photo states that
he provided: 'Kodaks & Photo Supplies."
F. L. HOUGHTON, 1909.

BELOW LEFT

In contrast to the above. This photograph from the album "Through Canada's North
Land" shows two Edwardian ladies and child studying a Cree woman and child.
ROBERT J. FLAHERTY, 1911.

"The Bride." A "Home Portrait Photographer's" picture of a young bride on her sunny wedding-day in Victoria, BC.

HENRY UPPERTON KNIGHT, 1920.

As the snow melts in the spring, a young Indian mother of Mingan, Quebec, on the north shore of the St Lawrence, opposite Anticosti Island, poses with her child. Her hat is in the Naskapi style.
KATE M.WILSON, 1906.

"The Siwash Madonna." A memorable photograph taken near Edmonton, Alberta. The Siwash were neither Northwest Coast nor Prairie Indians; they were Plateau Indians and usually lived no farther north than southern BC.
ROBERT W. LETT, 1922.

"Rt. Hon. David Lloyd George and Hon. Mederic Martin, Mayor of Montreal." In spite of the somewhat defiant poses here, the former Prime Minister of Britain had a rapturous reception during his 1923 tour of the United States and Canada. He sailed from Southampton to New York and then travelled by train to Montreal. During this journey numerous unscheduled stops were made along the way, for the crowds wanted to see Britain's war-time leader who had played an important part in the peace settlement. In Canada, he was fascinated by the extent to which radio had developed, far ahead, apparently, of the BBC which had been set up in Britain only the year before. As he headed west by train, he listened to radio bulletins about his own progress.

RICE STUDIOS LTD., 1923.

KALOMA.

COPYRIGHT. CANADA.
1914.
BY M. L. PRESSLER.
1914.

"Kaloma," one of only three nudes in the Collection, each with a suitably exotic-
sounding name. They may have been artists' models, or could they have been a belated
hint of the Naughty Nineties in frosty still Victorian Canada?

M. L. PRESSLER, 1914.

"Dr Bell and Party at the Home of the Telephone." It was a pensive Alexander Graham Bell, who, on this November day, had been present at the unveiling of a massive granite monument to himself at Brantford, Ontario. In another photograph he posed with "the man who laid the telephone line into the Bell Homestead". Here, his wife (Mabel Hubbard) is on the left. She was deaf since the age of four and became one of the first children in America to lip-read. Dr Bell's work with the deaf led to the invention of the telephone.

EDWARD P. PARK, 1906.

"On the Tote Road," somewhere in BC. A mysterious and evocative photograph. Who were they? Where were they going? Had they been made homeless? Most likely they were trekking to a mining camp.

RICHARD BROADBRIDGE, 1911.

"The Old Voyageur" photographed near Georgian Bay, Ontario.

JOHN WITHERSPOON BALD, 1901.

On the Tote Road

Copyright Canada.
1911   R. Broadwick.

71

"Morley Beaver and Friend" (LEFT) and "Gussie Goodstonie and Friend(s)." Their clothing suggests Plains Indians and their hair styles Cree. Originally the Cree were the Indians of the northern forests. There were widely separated bands who shared a common language.
BYRON HARMON, 1907.

"Benediction of the Blessed Sacrament, St. Anne's Convent, Quamichan, 1912." The participants seem to be mainly Indians, dressed in their Sunday best.
M. W. THOMPSTONE, 1912.

"Reception of the Papal Delegate, Chatham, N.B., June 8, 1914."
J. Y. MERCEREAU, 1914.

"Nearing the Bishop's Palace."
J. Y. MERCEREAU, 1914.

"Corpus Christi Procession, Montreal, 1917."
ARTHUR S. KUNZE, 1917.

"Drying fish." Near Kenora, Ontario, a fish has been hung to dry in the tree, while the skins of birds, probably herons or grebes, dry over the fire.
C. G. LINDE, 1912.

"Mending His Canoe". An Indian, probably Ojibwa, mends his birchbark canoe near Kenora, Ontario. The Ojibwa made extensive use of birchbark, and canoes such as this were used in the harvesting of wild rice.
C. G. LINDE, 1912.

"Men's bones found at Weston, Ont, April 28, 1911." No one knew why there should be bones in this place at Weston, now part of Toronto. It may have been an Indian burial ground. Such photographs allow for endless speculation.
GERALD KNOTHÉ, 1911.

A young Winnipeg boy attempts to "fix" his dad's camera – a folding rollfilm model.
The hammer is a humorous touch. This is the only photograph of a camera among the
recently discovered photographs.

Cameras were, by now, widely available. In Eaton's *Fall and Winter Catalogue* of 1898–9 seventeen camera models were advertised, from the Eureka No. 2 Kodak at $3.50 to the No. 4 Cartridge Kodak at $27.50. The latter could take cartridge or glass plates, and a wide-angle lens was available for a further $5.00.
JAY LAFAYETTE, 1915.

The Hon John Sebastian Helmcken emigrated to Canada from England in 1850 to become a surgeon for the Hudson's Bay Company. He was appointed a Justice of the Peace in Prince Rupert when a dispute erupted between the miners and the Indians. In 1856 he was elected to the Assembly of the Vancouver Island colony, the beginning of his political career. Most importantly, he was one of the three negotiators who brought British Columbia into Confederation in 1871. Although Helmcken had initially been opposed, once he was convinced that BC could be linked with the rest of Canada by rail he changed his mind. It was largely due to his efforts that the building of the transcontinental railway was made a condition of BC's entry. Canada's sixth highest waterfall, in Wells Gray Provincial Park, is named in tribute to him.

WALTER M. BAER, 1917.

ABOVE RIGHT

"The Sifton Reception." This reception was one of several held by Mrs Sifton in Edmonton in 1912. It was obviously an important social occasion, for it was attended by Princess Louise, wife of the Governor-General (and daughter-in-law of Queen Victoria), and their daughter Princess Patricia of Connaught. Clifford Sifton, Laurier's Minister of the Interior, was largely responsible for the policy of massive immigration in the early years of this century. The buildings of a rapidly growing Edmonton seem to be encroaching on this tranquil garden-party scene.

MCDERMID LTD., 1912.

BELOW RIGHT

"Gathering of the Boilermakers" – all hats and smiles. This photo is cloth-backed, as was sometimes done to strengthen the photograph.

GALBRAITH PHOTO CO., 1905.

Copyright, Canada, 1912
by McDermid Ltd. Edmonton.

"Arrival of Li Hung Chang, Chinese Viceroy at Vancouver, BC." The Viceroy was completing his 1896 world tour. He had been present at the Coronation of Tsar Nicholas II of Russia, had been received by Emperor Wilhelm of Germany, had had an audience with Queen Victoria, and had met Grover Cleveland, President of the United States. To complete his journey, the six-feet tall Viceroy visited Vancouver. The foggy day was brightened by "silken coats of diverse colours sported by Chinamen of high degree". Later, in 1898, he was a signatory to the convention leasing Kowloon to the British. By 1914 British Columbia would have an Asiatic population of 40,000.
JOHN WALLACE JONES, 1896.

ABOVE RIGHT
This cow-girl, perfectly attired in fringed skirt and stetson, appeared at a fair in 1920.
JOHN A. BROWN, 1920.

BELOW RIGHT
"Son Eminence, Le Cardinal Bégin" of Quebec.
MARCEL ALFRED MONTMINY, 1914.

ABOVE
"Indian Picnic at W. S. Piper's Farm, July 20th, 1920," Thunder Bay, Ontario.
WILLIAM S. PIPER, 1920.

ABOVE RIGHT
"Farewell to Government House. The Last State Dinner. 29th April 1912." The residence, on
the southwest corner of Simcoe and King was demolished in 1912 to make way for railway
expansion. The next Government House was built at Chorley Park in 1915. Such elegance was
a far cry from the "canvas house" of the early nineteenth century, for then Government House
had been a tent. John Ross Robertson was owner and publisher of Toronto's *Evening Telegram*.
JOHN ROSS ROBERTSON, 1912.

BELOW RIGHT
"Farewell to Government House. The 'Last Dance'. 29th April, 1912." This is one of the few
action shots in the Collection.
JOHN ROSS ROBERTSON, 1912.

FAREWELL TO GOVERNMENT HOUSE.
THE LAST STATE DINNER.
29TH APRIL 1912.

COPYRIGHT CANADA 1912.
BY J. ROSS ROBERTSON.
TORONTO.

FAREWELL TO GOVERNMENT HOUSE.
THE LAST DANCE. 29TH APRIL 1912.

COPYRIGHT CANADA 1912.
BY J. ROSS ROBERTSON.
TORONTO.

SHEELOR PHOTO.

ALL
TOGETHER

ABOVE
A detail from "Bernard Avenue from the
Presbyterian Church Tower, Kelowna, B.C., 1910."

G. H. E. HUDSON, 1910.

LEFT
Dawson City, Yukon Territory. A fascinating
photograph of Dawson in 1916, a detail of which is
shown here. The photograph is one and a half
metres (five feet) long.
F. W. SHEELOR, 1916.

"Winnipeg, corner of Portage Avenue and Main Street, 1872." Sometimes photographs were deposited to register copyright years after they were taken, which is why this early view of Winnipeg is in a collection dating from 1895 to 1924.
ROBERT CHAMBERLAIN, 1910.

BELOW
A panoramic view of a prosperous, thriving Winnipeg in 1913, one in a series. This is a detail of a photograph which is about a metre (three and half feet) long. At its incorporation in 1873, the population of Winnipeg was 1,869. By 1914 this figure had reached 203,255. Prosperity was in the air. There had been a bumper wheat crop in 1901 and Winnipeg was a centre for moving cattle to eastern markets. The city was no less than the financial, manufacturing and distribution centre for the West. But with the opening of the Panama Canal in 1914, distribution patterns changed and a depression set in.
REMBRANDT STUDIOS, 1913.

"Drawing Room, Royal Alexandra Hotel." In 1907 Winnipeg could offer first class – and elegant – accomodation to visitors. The regal old hotel stood at Main Street and Higgins Avenue until it was demolished in 1972.
THE CONSOLIDATED STATIONERY COMPANY, 1907.

"Ruins from Queen's Hotel." On 19 April 1904 Toronto experienced a spectacular and disastrous fire. It began in the E. & S. Currie neckware company, located on the north side of Wellington Street between Yonge and Bay. The fire was whipped up by a strong north wind, and entire blocks were soon burning. The historic Queen's Hotel, which stood where the Royal York is now, was saved by staff, guests and the public who battled for hours using blankets soaked in bathtubs and every other means. Firemen rushed to Toronto on special trains from as far away as Buffalo, London and Peterborough. Unbelievably, no lives were lost, but thousands of people experienced temporary unemployment because 5.67 hectares (fourteen acres) of downtown Toronto was destroyed.

GALBRAITH PHOTO CO., 1904.

ABOVE LEFT

"R.C.M.P. Riding School. Erected 1888. Destroyed 1920." Where people went the Mounties followed. Sergeant Brinkworth was on hand to record the fire which destroyed this sturdy structure at Regina.

GEORGE WALTER BRINKWORTH, 1921.

BELOW LEFT

After the disastrous fire on 22 June 1908, Trois Rivières was in ruins. Only one street survived the fire, Rue des Ursulines, where today some buildings date from the seventeenth and eighteenth centuries. Major fires were common in Canadian towns and cities at the turn of the century. Buildings were constructed largely of wood, fire-fighting facilities were scarce, and water pressure low. The Trois Rivières fire is recorded in an album of twenty-four photographs entitled *"Souvenir de L'Incendie de Trois-Rivières"*.

P. FORTUNAT PINSONNEAULT, 1908.

"General view of Halifax showing damage to buildings not burned. Looking west." This long panoramic view is one of several showing the result of the Halifax explosion on 6 December 1917, a strange echo of the scenes of devastation on the European battlefields across the water. It was the greatest man-made explosion known prior to the Atomic bomb.

The Bedford Basin at Halifax, Nova Scotia was a gathering place for convoys during the First World War, so ships could cross the Atlantic in safety. The French munitions ship *Mont Blanc* had arrived to join a convoy when there was a collision with a Belgian relief ship, the *Imo*. Fire broke out, the crews abandoned ship, and the ships drifted. Then the deadly combination of explosives and chemicals blew up. At least 1,400 people were killed outright and about 600 died later. Another 9,000 were injured and 200 were blinded. The ships' crews survived. The north end of Halifax was demolished, the buildings near the waterfront being blasted from their foundations.

W. G. MACLAUGHLIN, 1917.

ABOVE RIGHT
"Inaugural Meeting City Council Toronto Jan. 9, 1911" in the building now known as Old City Hall, affectionately preserved by Toronto's citizens.

F. W. MICKLETHWAITE, 1911.

BELOW RIGHT
"St Dunstan's Cathedral. Burning of Sydney St. Side at 3 o'clock, A.M., March 8, 1913. Charlottetown, P.E.I." St. Dunstan's Basilica has arisen on this spot. Disasters such as fires were often photographed, because they were news and drama.

STIFF PHOTO, 1913.

Church fire at St Anne de Beaupré, Quebec on 29 March 1922. The religious statues stand, strangely, in the snow, a safe distance from the church which was completely burnt out. Since 1658 this town has been visited by millions of people seeking cures at the shrine there.
W. B. EDWARDS, 1922.

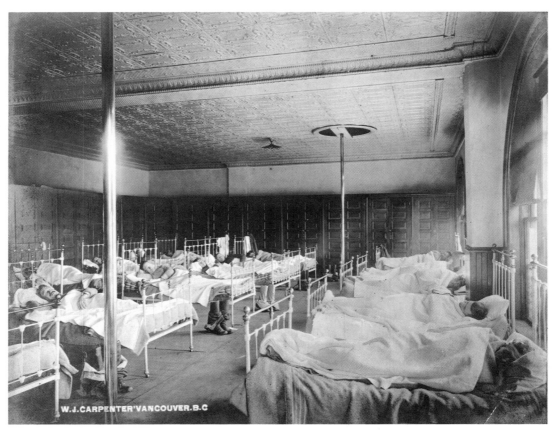

"Vancouver Firemen's Sleeping Apartment." Trousers and boots poised for action and brass poles gleaming, the firemen pretend to sleep while their picture is being taken. By 1900 Vancouver had invested in a well-equipped fire department. Almost immediately after the city's incorporation in 1886, it had been wiped out by a fire.
WILLIAM J. CARPENTER, 1910.

"Opening New Parliament Buildings at Victoria, BC, Feb. 10 1898. Arrival Lieut.-Governor and Suite." The opening took place on a wet and misty day, which partially obscured the view of British Columbia's new Parliament Buildings. They were expected to cost $600,000 – more than one-third of the province's annual revenue. The final cost was over $900,230. It has often been said that Victoria is more English than England. However, when the first Premier, J. H. Turner, finally retired he realized his dream and went to Kew Gardens in England.

JOHN WALLACE JONES, 1898.

"First St. and Bruce Ave. South Porcupine Ont." Gold was discovered in the Porcupine – Kirkland Lake – Timmins region in 1903. Towns like South Porcupine sprang up, sometimes complete with their own Photo Studio, advertising "Portraits and Supplies".

ARTHUR THOMKINSON, 1913.

93

"Transferring Real Estate in Nova Scotia." A team of forty oxen were needed to move this home.
WILLIAM HERBERT PERCY, 1913.

BELOW
"Montreal Harbour." An extraordinary composite photograph of Montreal Harbour in 1920. The composer
of this scene was determined to show that Montreal was a thriving metropolis, and he succeeded. There is
action everywhere, even in the sky where airplanes and seagulls have been painted in. The city fathers
noted that Montreal was "one of the largest seaports in the world" and liked to refer to 19 August 1920
when there had been forty-six ocean liners docked there. In the 1920s it was the world's greatest grain port.
J. A. MILLAR, 1920.

71248 (13.)

"Digby Wharves." A summer's day at Digby, Nova Scotia.
Ferries left from here for New Brunswick.
PAUL YATES, 1906.

A small Ontario town in 1905. The photographer, James Esson (1853–1933?), produced a picture essay of life in Preston, Ontario – his home town – in an album of seventeen views. Many are of the hotel gardens and mineral springs, but there are a few everyday and working scenes.

All in all it is a very appealing look at what seems to be a neat and well-organized little town. Esson's work was highly regarded, and some called him the "Wilson of Canada" after an internationally famous Scottish photographer of that name.

JAMES ESSON, 1905.

FROM PLACE TO PLACE

"This is the first photo of the first train as she steamed over the Bridge and touched the fertile soil of Edmonton. This is also the first train that crossed the South Saskatchewan River. J. G. Entwistle, Eng. & N. Dohm, fireman. Oct. 20, 1902." Everyone wanted to share in an event of such importance to communities on both sides of the river.

GEORGE O. CLARK, 1904.

"Only a stream divides Detroit and the Border Cities." The "stream" is the Detroit River. Windsor, Ontario is on the right and Detroit on the left. Windsor's position on the river and so close to a major US city ensured its success as a manufacturing and industrial centre.

BORDER CHAMBER OF COMMERCE, 1918.

"Opening of Navigation at Port Arthur, May 2, 1912, 20 boat(s) carrying over 5,000,000 Bsl of wheat. View No. 1." The boats are following one another in a channel cut by an ice-breaker.

J. F. COOKE, 1912.

"Crossing the moon's glory path." A tranquil scene at Saskatoon, Saskatchewan. Saskatoon had been founded in 1883 as a temperance colony, but after twenty years there were still only 113 inhabitants. The railway went through in 1908 and settlers from the Ukraine, Britain, Germany and Scandinavia poured in. When it came time to chose a permanent capital for Saskatchewan – Regina was considered to be temporary – Saskatoon made a determined bid, as did several other cities. This meant chartered trains and special banquets for prominent people, but in the end the politicians decided to stay in Regina.

PETER MCKENZIE, 1910.

"The wreck of the artillery train at Enterprise, Ontario." The wreck, on 9 June 1903, was an event in Enterprise, a small Ontario town north-east of Napanee. The local photographer, a woman, recorded it and sent her album of eighteen photographs to Ottawa to register copyright.

We do not know what caused Engine No. 5 to become derailed, although it may have been a cow on the Belleville-Ottawa line. The train carried soldiers, gun carriages, and the horses to pull them.

No. 16 – The Wreck of the artillery train at Enterprise, Ont
June 9th 1903

The Militia sternly guarded the wreck, as the local populace looked on, fascinated with this sudden drama in their quiet lives.

No. 18 – The Wreck of the artillery train at
June 9th 1903

One hot and weary soldier has hung his pith helmet on the signal box. The local farmers found a perfect seat from which to watch the action. For entertainment value a train wreck couldn't be beat.

HARRIETT AMELIA MAY, 1903.

"On Kootenay Lake." Working steamships played an enormous and little-known role in opening up the country, especially – suprisingly – on the large lakes and rivers of the prairies. Even the railways had their own fleets of steamships to keep goods moving.

E. A. BUCHHOLZ, 1908.

"Grand Trunk Car Shops, London, Ont." A town was indeed fortunate when the railway favoured it in this way with a source of permanent employment. The Grand Trunk Railway, incorporated in 1852–53, was the main railway system of Ontario and Quebec. In 1859 the main line was extended to Sarnia, and in the same year the branch to London was opened. It later became part of the Canadian National Railway.

JAMES M. GOWAN, 1909.

"Canadian Pacific Railway Viaduct" across the Oldman River at Lethbridge, Alberta.
"Length one mile 847 feet. Height 307 feet." This made it the longest
and highest railway bridge in Canada.
A. RAFTON-CANNING, 1909.

"The S.S. *Cheslakee* wrecked at Van Anda," on Texada Island near Powell River, BC, January 1913.
The *Cheslakee* gently sinks, as goods are removed.
WALTER JAMES ELLIS, 1913.

"The Rotary Snow-Plow in action", a turn-of-the-century invention for removing snow from railway tracks, which received much publicity.
TOWNE & THORPE, 1912.

ABOVE LEFT
"A Sleigh Motor Cycle." Travelling in style on an early Harley Davidson, complete with skis.
Harley Davidsons, with their always strikingly individual character, were first made in 1903.
JOHN G. DICKSON, 1914.

BELOW LEFT
"The Bridal Car." Cars soon became a common sight, and a most desirable mode of transport for a special day.
HENRY CHARLES WHITE, 1922.

"Panoramic Auto Show Exhibition." A fascinating view of a 1913 auto show in Vancouver. Customers could study the Albions, Federals and other makes of cars from the comfort of deeply upholstered chairs, seated amongst palms and ornamental trees. Tires are prominently displayed, for in those early years one could expect a flat tire every few miles.
CANADA PHOTO CO., 1913.

BELOW RIGHT
"Launching of the *Toronto*" from The Bertram Co. Ship Yard, Toronto. Bertrams was on the corner of Bathurst Street and Niagara, near Queen's Wharf.
WILLIAM THOMPSON FREELAND, 1898.

AT THE

"Launching of the Toronto"

ENTERED ACCORDING TO ACT OF THE PARLIAMENT OF CANADA, IN THE YEAR 1898,
BY W. T. FREELAND, AT THE DEPARTMENT OF AGRICULTURE

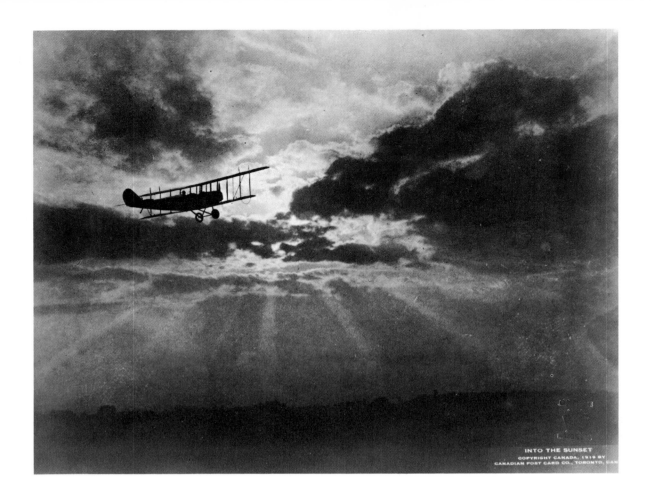

INTO THE SUNSET
COPYRIGHT CANADA, 1919 BY
CANADIAN POST CARD CO., TORONTO, CAN

"Into the Sunset," one in a series.
Others were titled "The Silver Lining," and "Evening Sunset."
CANADIAN POST CARD CO., 1919.

ABOVE RIGHT

Steamboat skirting the Lachine Rapids in 1923. This dramatic river trip was
much photographed. The rapids were so turbulent in Cartier's time that he
was forced to abandon his plan to go farther west up the St Lawrence. The
Lachine Canal was built in 1824.
SYDNEY JACK HAWYARD, 1923.

BELOW RIGHT

The Quebec Bridge in 1907. It was the greatest cantilever bridge in North
America when it was built. Spans fell during the first two attempts, but it was
finally opened in 1917. Soldiers stood on the pylons to guard it during the
war. The large rocks in the foreground distort the scale of the photograph, for
the bridge was immense.
E. R. KINLOCK, 1907.

Entered according to Act of Parliment of Canada, in the year 1907, by E.R.Kinloch, of the Department of Agriculture.

48
8-14-0

"Entrance to Pictou Harbour."
This was an exceptionally well protected harbour on the north side of Nova Scotia.
WILLIAM M. MUNRO, 1906.

A line up of early cars at Alberni Quay, Vancouver Island.
LEONARD FRANK, 1912.

RIGHT
In 1912 Thomas W. Wilby and his driver crossed Canada in his car the "Pathfinder". They had dipped the
back wheels in the Atlantic at Halifax and the front wheels in the Pacific at Vancouver. Wilby was
determined to establish a highway which crossed Canada from coast to coast – the All Red Route. Along the
way they had picked up banners from the towns and cities they passed through.
RICHARD BROADBRIDGE, 1912.

"Munitions Worker making Shells" in a Toronto factory. During the First World War Canada produced hundreds of millions of dollars worth of munitions. As more men went to war, a shortage of labour developed; the workers left were able to demand more money and better working conditions, and organized themselves into trade unions.

STONE LIMITED, 1915.

EARNING A CRUST

"Fishing Boats – The Mosquito Fleet – Prince Rupert, BC."
Prince Rupert, on the coast opposite the north end of
Vancouver Island is near the mouth of the Skeena river. From
the earliest days it has had a fishing fleet.
DUNCAN C. MCRAE, 1916.

"The Harvest of the Sea" at Prince Rupert.
M. M. STEPHENS, 1913.

"Middleton Farm No. 1." From a series depicting ploughing by steam tractor
on the prairies near Saskatoon.
BENJAMIN. P. SKEWIS, 1912.

"Living Models in Plumbing Fixtures." An early advertising picture from Halifax, Nova Scotia, one of a series promoting plumbing fixtures. Here the models are looking at the "Daisy" Heater.
WILLIAM STAIRS, SON AND MORROW LIMITED, 1921.

"Ready to Break".
A. E. BROWN, 1912.

"Laura Elevator Wreck No. 1." A grain elevator has collapsed on to the
railway tracks near Saskatoon.
BENJAMIN P. SKEWIS, 1911.

"Prairie Valley, Summerland, BC" in the Okanagan Valley, one of Canada's most
important fruit-growing centres. Here the orchards are
beautifully laid out in a perfect setting.
G. H. E. HUDSON, 1909.

"High Rigging." The photographer often managed to have a lady present to admire the proceedings when lumberjacks were photographed. Forestry was first established in BC by the Hudson's Bay Company, when they built a mill at Esquimalt. After some ups and downs, export trade in timber was growing by the turn of the century, and Canada's forests started disappearing.

COMMERCIAL PHOTO CO., 1918.

"Onion Crop. 1909. Grown by J. Casaro & Sons. Kelowna, BC."
A satisfying moment when the crop, successfully grown, is about to be despatched.
S. GRAY, 1909.

"The Prospector" near Vancouver, B.C.
T. BENTLEY, 1920.

Fur industries in Prince Edward Island.
The black foxes were residents of a much photographed fur farm.
In some of the photographs the foxes are hand-fed, and seem more like pets than commodities.
J. B. ROMBOROUGH, 1921.

This little creature was apparently "Canada's First Persian Lamb," only two days and nine hours old.
W. H. TIDEMARSH, 1914.

"Stope in cliff mine, Rossland, B.C." This underground photograph was taken with the difficult and dangerous flashlight powder that had been invented in the 1880s.
EDWARDS BROS., 1897.

"Packing Room at Hillcrest, Kentville, Nova Scotia, No. 6."
A. L. HARDY, 1911.

"Waiting." The farm girl of 1900 who posed for this photograph was probably of
Dutch or German extraction.
E. J. ROWLEY, 1900.

"Power Spraying, No. 14," Kentville, Nova Scotia.
A. L. HARDY, 1912.

"Picking apples in the orchard of Mr. S. L. Pridham, Kelowna, B.C."
G. H. E. HUDSON, 1910.

CROWN AND COUNTRY

"The Second Charlottetown Detachment who volunteered for Service with The Canadian Contingent for the War in South Africa." Even tiny Prince Edward Island was represented in the Canadian Contingent. The decision was made by the government to raise "not more than 1,000 troops" on 13 October. These troops were recruited with unbelievable speed and sailed from Quebec on 30 October 1899.
GEORGE H. COOK, 1900.

The Living Union Jack Picture

Witnesses

Newton D. Galbreaith

Jas Gadsby

Certified to be the Photograph referred to in the accompanying application for Copyright

Sara Elizabeth Charlton

By W. Bruce
Atty

Hamilton Ont. Nov. 28th 1898

Rifle Drill on board the SS *Monterey* for members of the Strathcona Horse. The Canadian government had not intended to become involved in the South African War, but public demand forced them to raise two "official" contingents. Most costs were picked up by the imperial authorities, although the Strathcona Horse was funded by a private individual. In all, 8,472 Canadians fought in the South African War (1899–1902).
HENRY DUNSFORD, 1900.

ABOVE LEFT
"The Living Union Jack Picture."
SARA ELIZABETH CHARLTON, 1898.

BELOW LEFT
"Soldiers of the Queen". Queen Victoria with some of her soldiers in a commemorative of the South African War. Less than two months before her death she was to review at Windsor some of the Canadian troops who had fought in South Africa.
JOSEPH C. CLARKE, 1900.

Queen Victoria's third son, the Duke of Connaught, was Governor-General of Canada from 1911 to 1916. In 1918 his daughter, Princess Patricia (on his right), became Honorary Colonel-in-Chief of Princess Patricia's Canadian Light Infantry Battalion. In the First World War, it was the Princess Pat's, the core of experienced soldiers, who first carried the badge of Canada on to the battlefield at Flanders.

ALFRED GEORGE PITTAWAY, 1913.

RIGHT

The Duke and Duchess of Cornwall and York, later George V and Queen Mary, in the ferny conservatory of Government House, Ottawa. They toured Canada on the return journey from a visit to Australia to open Parliament there. The Duchess is still in mourning, for Queen Victoria had died earlier in the year.

WILLIAM NOTMAN AND SON, 1901.

"Scotch Highlanders, 78th Regiment", near Bear River, Nova Scotia.
R. H. HARRIS, 1913.

"Inspection by the King of the Canadian troops on Salisbury Plain." When the first Canadian troops arrived in England, Kitchener felt they were not sufficiently trained and wanted to incorporate them with British troops. This suggestion was fiercely and successfully resisted by Colonel Sam Hughes, Canada's Minister of Militia, who by the strength of his own personality had raised large numbers of the troops. The Canadians were forced, discouragingly, to winter on Salisbury Plain, where in the spring they were reviewed by George V before leaving for the battlefields.
GOODWINS LIMITED, 1917.

"The Farewell." A calm, almost nonchalant embarkation by train, at Montreal.
A. A. CHESTERFIELD, 1915.

COPY DEPOSITED NO. 34917

"Civilised warfare." This sardonic heading sums up the photographers' disgust with the war. The men were probably soldiers. (*Top left*) Battalions in trenches prior to going over the top. (*Top right*) German prisoners carrying their wounded. (*Above left*) Scene 3/4 hour after a shell burst. (*Above, right*) Shell-burst.
WILLIAM PERCY KIBBLER, JOHN PRISSOM, HOWARD KEARNLEY GOODWIN, 1918.

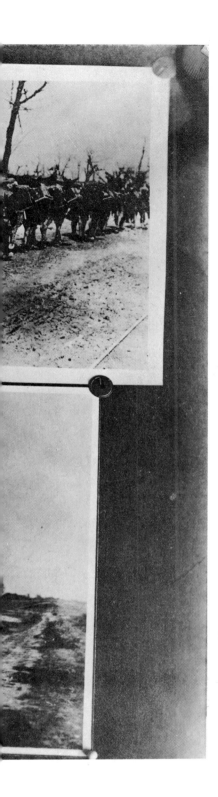

THE SOLDIER'S SWEETHEART.

I see a blood-red moon in Europe's sky—
The earth turns crimson as her heroes die—
And while brave men fall victims of the war,
We mothers, wives and sweethearts cry, "What for?"

"Defender" You can't beat it cause I am setting on it

JAY LAFAYETTE
486 PORTAGE AVE.
WINNIPEG

For the photographer of this picture, a woman, the war was very real. No one knows
who she was or why she was at the battlefields. She was not one of the accredited
Canadian photographers, although she may have been a nurse or an ambulance driver. In
October 1920 she deposited for copyright her album of photographs entitled "War
Studies by Olive Edis".

It was during the second battle of Ypres in 1915 that the Canadian medical officer,
Colonel John Macrae, wrote "In Flanders Fields". The Poem was written between the
arrival of batches of wounded men, and in sight of recent war graves around which
poppies had grown up, and where his best friend lay buried. McCrae himself died in a
military hospital in 1918. Each year a special bouquet of poppies is placed on his grave.

OLIVE EDIS, 1920.

LEFT
"Defender" representing the women left behind, with the coy remark "You can't beat it
cause I am sitting on it." Canadian women were soon filling men's jobs in agriculture
and industry, including munitions factories; but they still did not have the vote.

JAY LAFAYETTE, 1915.

"Inspector-General Sir A. W. Currie with 'Muggins' of Red Cross Fame." One in a series showing the first Canadian commander with a Red Cross mascot. Currie had been appointed Commander of the Canadian Corps in 1917. Although a militia officer before the war, he was not a professional soldier; he had been a real estate agent. This convinced some Canadians that it was not necessary to have a standing army in peacetime, if an amateur could take over so capably.

HENRY S. HENDERSON, VICTORIA BOOK AND STATIONARY COMPANY, 1919.

"Col. Barker, VC, in one of the captured German aeroplanes against which he fought his last battle." Major Barker, a Canadian in the RAF was awarded his VC for action on 27 October 1918 during the Valenciennes battle. The sky was full of German planes when he dived into their midst and enemy planes began falling to the ground. He was hit several times, losing consciousness once, but each time recovered and shot down more German Fokkers, of the type he was photographed in here. He finally crash-landed behind his own lines and recovered. Major General McNaughton, who was present with thousands of other troops on the ground below, said, "The spectacle of this attack was the most magnificent encounter of any sort I have ever witnessed. The ancient performances of the gladiators in the Roman arena were far outclassed. . ."
Major Barker was killed in a flying accident near Ottawa in 1930.

CANADIAN POST CARD COMPANY, 1919.

"The Prince of Wales at Dixie." A candid snapshot of the Prince near Toronto.
This adored Prince of Wales toured Canada in August and November of 1919.
There was a rapturous welcome for a charming young man who was heir to the
throne. It was also an emotional release at war's end.
WILLIAM JAMES WILCOX, 1919.

"View on the Speed River, Preston, Ontario."
JAMES ESSON, 1905.

HAVING FUN

"Bluenose leading the Elimination race" in 1921. *Bluenose* was never beaten, and this distinguished vessel is depicted on the Canadian dime. In 1942, sadly, she was sold and became a freighter in the West Indies, only to be wrecked off Haiti in 1946.

W. R. MACASKILL, 1921.

"Ottawa Hockey Team N.H. AssTN World Champions and Stanley Cup Holders."
Well satisfied smiles from the winners of the Stanley Cup in 1911.
ALFRED GEORGE PITTAWAY, 1911.

A pin-up of a girl hockey player in 1904, one of a series. The short skirt, carefully
turned up in each photo, hinted at naughtiness.
WILLIAM ELISHA MAY, 1904.

"S.S. *Okanagan* & Kelowna's lake frontage."
G. H. E. HUDSON, 1910.

"The start of race, Kelowna, BC, 1909." A polo pony race was part of the festivities during the 1909 regatta.
Today there are two regattas every year at Kelowna, which have won international acclaim.
G. H. E. HUDSON, 1909.

143

"Tobagganing Park Slide." The slide was lit up so the fun could continue in the evening.
WILLIAM NOTMAN AND SON, 1910.

"Montreal Curling Group." The Scottish heritage in Canada is very strong.
WILLIAM NOTMAN AND SON, 1905.

Advertising card for Montreal's Théâtre des Nouveautés.
LAPRES & LAVERGNE, 1904.

"The Kermesse at Quebec." The patriotic finale of the *kermesse* or annual carnival.
W. B. EDWARDS, 1919.

"The 'Tigers' of Hamilton." It was early days for the Hamilton Tiger Cats, when they posed to have their picture taken at half time.
ALEXANDER MCKENZIE CUNNINGHAM, 1906.

An animal trainer with the other members of his circus act. The dogs were trained to complete this set piece by placing their front paws on the rumps of the zebras. The latter, in this case, are crossbred horses and zebras.
JOHN A. BROWN, 1920.

"Wishing you a Happy New Century." A humorous greeting at the turn of the century.
FRED HACKING, 1900.

"The Ice Palace, Montreal Winter Carnival, 1910." At the turn of the century winter carnivals usually featured an ice palace and celebrations were concluded with a display of fireworks in it. Montreal's ice palace of 1883, the first one in North America, was constructed of 10,000 blocks of ice, each weighing 227 kilograms (500 pounds). Crystal clear lake ice was preferred. Ice palaces following this became larger and more elaborate.

Entered according to Act of the Parliament of Canada, in the year 1910, by S. H. N. Kennedy, at the Department of Agriculture.

"Mountain climbing on Snow Shoes."
SAMUEL H. N. KENNEDY, 1910.

"Cyclorama of the Canadian National Exhibition, 1919."
WILLIAM THOMPSON FREELAND, 1919.

W. George Beers had taken the disorganized game that the Indians played and had written a rule book. He decided to make lacrosse the national game of Canada, although there is no evidence that this was ever done officially. Montreal had a French team, an English team, and an Irish Catholic team, while Toronto had an Irish Protestant team. With teams organized along these lines, encounters were often violent, which probably led to the decline of the sport. The most eagerly attended games were those played against Indian teams, who remained highly skilled in what had been their game. By 1910 hockey had replaced snow-shoeing as the favourite winter sport and baseball had replaced lacrosse as a summer sport.
PATRICK JOHN GORDON, 1903.

ABOVE RIGHT
"'A Dog Team', South Porcupine, Ont." A lady from the gold camp taking the air.
W. J. BROWN, 1912.

BELOW RIGHT
Stunts with cars became a crowd-drawing attraction at country fairs.
MCDERMID STUDIOS LIMITED, 1923.

"A dog team" South Porcupine, Ont

WORLD'S RECORD JUMP 73 ft. 2"
BY J. PAUL WELCH
EDMONTON, ALTA, MAY 24th, 1923
Copyrighted McDermid Studios Ltd.

COPY DEPOSITED NO,

Scene in the Butcha

The Quebec Tercentenary in 1908 was celebrated with pageants and festivities. This is a detail from the "Second Pageant. Champlain receives his commission from Henri IV." On the Plains of Abraham with the mighty St Lawrence as an incomparable backdrop, nine pageants depicting events from three hundred years of Quebec's history were acted out. The photographer had a handy order form on the back of each photograph and presumably sold these photographs, which were a metre (three-and-a-half feet) long to the beautifully costumed "cast of 5,000". It was noted at the time that those who took part were often descendants of the original settlers.

H. O. DODGE, 1908.

LEFT

"Butchardt Gardens." A panoramic view almost one metre (three feet) long. The gardens had been opened in 1909 by Mrs Jennie Butchardt, whose husband's lime quarry had left an ugly scar. The beautiful gardens she created in the quarry quickly became a West Coast showpiece.

JOHN WOOD, 1920.

The yacht *Shamrock* racing on Lake Ontario in 1898. Yacht-racing on Lake Ontario attracted much participation and interest before the turn of the century. The first lake yacht-racing association had been formed in 1884, and the Royal Hamilton Yacht Club received its charter in 1894.
ROBERT DUNCAN CO., 1899.

"Ski Jumping".
WILLIAM NOTMAN AND SON, 1905

SELECTED READING

Many sources have been useful in the preparation of this work, including issues of *Canadian Geographic* and *National Geographic Magazine*. Of the books I would particularly like to mention the following.

Cavell, Edward, *Sometimes a Great Nation*. Altitude Publishing, Banff, 1984.

Coe, Brian, and Hanworth-Booth, Mark, *A Guide to Early Photographic Processes*. Hurtwood Press in association with The Victoria and Albert Museum, London, 1983.

Creighton, Donald, *Canada's First Century*. Macmillan of Canada, Toronto, 1970.

Granatstein, J. L., Abella, Irving M., Bercuson, David J., Brown, R. Craig, and Neatby, H. Blair, *Twentieth Century Canada*. McGraw-Hill Ryerson Limited, 1983.

Greenhill, Ralph, and Birrell, Andrew, *Canadian Photography, 1839–1920*. The Coach House Press, Toronto, 1979.

Jensen, Oliver, Kerr, Joan Patterson, and Belsky, Murray, *American Album*. American Heritage Publishing Co. Ltd., 1968.

McLaren-Turner, Patricia (ed.), *Canadian Studies, British Library Occasional Papers 1*. The British Library, London, 1984.

Munro, Iain R., *Canadians and the World Wars*. Wiley Publishers of Canada Limited, Toronto, 1979.

Stacey, C. P., *Canada and the Age of Conflict, Volume 1: 1867–1921*. Macmillan of Canada, Toronto, 1977.

Wilson, James, *Canada's Indians*. Minority Rights Group, London, rev. edn. 1982.

AUTHOR'S ACKNOWLEDGEMENTS

Researching this book in the unique collection of Canadian photographs at the British Library has for me been a wonderful – indeed incomparable – lesson in Canadian history. I would like to acknowledge the cooperation, assistance and encouragement of the following:

The Board and staff of the British Library, including Hugh Cobbe, Head of Publications; Dr Helen Wallis, Map Librarian; and especially Jim Egles, a curator in the English Language Section. It was under Jim's knowledgeable eye that the recently discovered Canadian photographs remained until incorporated into the system, and Jim has been most interested and helpful on all occasions.

Dr Patrick O'Neill of Mount Saint Vincent University, Halifax, who first discovered the extent of the Canadian Collection at the British Library has given me information and advice which has been very much appreciated.

Margaret Cooter and Barbara James, the two Canadian researchers who worked on the Collection at different times, have both been friendly and helpful. In addition, I must thank Margaret for her assistance with research, and also Rita West.

My brother, Ted Culp, first told me about the discovery at the British Library, and thus set off a happy sequence of events.

The following have given this project enthusiastic support, for which I am very grateful: William Hanna, Vice President of General Publishing; Ronald Whiting and Janet Liebster – and a special "thank you" to Janet Cooper of Hamlyn Publishing.

I would also like to thank my editor, Michael Stapleton, and designer Heather Sherratt.

INDEX OF PHOTOGRAPHERS

INDEX

ENDPAPER

The South African War was soon eclipsed by the First World War. This is a detail of a magnificent panoramic photograph, more than a metre (four feet) long, of the 23rd Battalion on 10 February 1915. They were part of the 2nd Canadian Expeditionary Force, and sailed in February with two other battalions. After arriving in England, all three battalions were drafted to the 1st Canadian Division. By the end of November 1915, of the men of the 23rd Battalion, twenty-eight were killed in action, nine died of wounds, four of disease, one was missing in action, and ninety-six were wounded.

PERCY E. MCDONALD, 1915.